DATE DUE

Art Center College of Design
Library
1700 Lida Street
Pasadena, Calif. 91103

42UP

42 UP

"Give Me the Child Until He Is Seven, and I Will Show You the Man"

A Book Based on Michael Apted's Award-Winning Documentary Series

Edited by BENNETT SINGER

THE NEW PRESS NEW YORK

42 up: "give me the child until he is seven, and I will show you the man: a book based
on Michael Apted's award-winning documentary series/edited by Bennett Singer;
introduction by Michael Apted; preface by Robert Coles; foreword by Roger Ebert.
        p.   cm.
    isbn 1-56584-465-3
    1. Children — Great Britain — Longitudinal studies. 2. Working class —
Great Britain — Longitudinal studies. 3. Children in motion pictures —
Great Britain. 4. Working class in motion pictures — Great Britain. 5. Documentary
    films — Great Britain. I. Singer, Bennett L. II. Apted, Michael.
HQ792.G7A18 1998
305.23'0941 — dc21   98-33636
                                                                         CIP

Published in the United States by The New Press, New York
Distributed by W. W. Norton & Company, Inc., New York

The New Press was established in 1990 as a not-for-profit alternative to the large,
commercial publishing houses currently dominating the book publishing industry.
The New Press operates in the public interest rather than for private gain,
and is committed to publishing, in innovative ways, works of educational, cultural,
and community value that are often deemed insufficiently profitable.

www.thenewpress.com

Printed in the United States of America

9 8 7 6 5 4 3 2 1

CONTENTS

Preface by Robert Coles   **7**

Foreword by Roger Ebert   **9**

Editor's Note   **12**

Introduction by Michael Apted   **13**

TONY   **17**

SUZY   **35**

SYMON   **47**

BRUCE   **59**

LYNN   **71**

NICK   **79**

SUE   **93**

PAUL   **105**

ANDREW   **117**

JACKIE   **127**

NEIL   **139**

Epilogue   **155**

PREFACE
by ROBERT COLES

Years ago, I was lucky indeed to study under and teach for Erik H. Erikson, a child psychoanalyst who insisted upon describing his academic knowledge as that of "human development." I remember once asking him about that particular phrase. His answer was brief, pointed: "It is what happens to all of us. We move across time—things happen to us and we grow, change, develop (whatever word you want to use)." I especially liked that modestly poetic notion of us as in motion, traveling over the years—a suggestive manner of thinking about life: a journey in which our ways get shaped in the course of our days. Even better, actually, is the film documentarian Michael Apted's wonderfully concise and unaffected way of regarding our experience of being alive—that single, small word "up," a huge statement held firmly high by two letters: life as an accumulation of years that take us forward, lift us away from our beginnings, and, inevitably, nearer to our last days, our concluding moments.

Of course, some of us, religiously minded, will invoke the imagery of a spiritual destination—"up" as a movement toward God and His realm, that "promised land" of heaven. Others, contemporary secularists, will want to resort to the confident categorizations of psychology, split our life's span into the various phases and stages, each a turf of sorts, with its particular demands, challenges, hazards—all of that a means, perhaps, of giving us at least the notion, if not conviction, that we have things under decided control. But Michael Apted is a film documentarian—an artist, that is. He puts himself out there, in that anthropological "field"—in the world of various individuals. He is open to those fellow human beings, eager to know them as children, follow them along as they grow, take on life, respond to it in ways surprising or not hard to guess as likely. He is, then, a psychological observer who is also a skilled student of our social and cultural values—all of that, however, folded unpretentiously but knowingly into a visionary dream: that with time and patience and the skills required to master a camera, to use it in the company of others, a broad and richly detailed and ever so revealing view of certain lives will be realized.

Needless to say, in the pages that follow, such a vision, recorded on film, is now offered us in a book—the words spoken by the boys and girls, the men and women Mr. Apted and his camera crew kept visiting across those seven-year cycles, and too, the pictures of those people, "stills" from all that footage: moments of appearance amidst the large flow of self-presentation that is collectively known as a person's life. In a sense, then, this book offers a transfer of sorts, within the documentary tradition—an opportunity, thereby, for us to stop and ponder (and savor) the ever-growing harvest of a documentarian's persistent efforts.

No question, those of us who have done documentary work in our own ways will be attracted to this book as we were attracted to Mr. Apted's films—here is an extraordinary commitment of talent, energy, skill to an idea that has become a continuing visual reality: creativity turned into a creation whose overall life now approaches a half-century duration. But surely this body of work belongs not only to film buffs, or to those social scientists who will justifiably be interested by (stand in awe of) what has been accomplished by this long-standing exploration of the life cycle. Rather, the rest of us, ordinary men and women who have been children, then teenagers, and then grown-ups (meaning full-fledged citizens of a country, and husbands and wives and lovers and workers and householders) will surely claim the right to learn from this determinedly loyal investigation of "time and being," as the existentialist philosophers would say it. In a society so beholden to manuals of all sorts, each telling us how to negotiate this or that "problem," or period of years, this book, like the successive films that enable it, gives us quite another perspective—a wide-eyed innocence that ironically owes its emergence to a thoroughgoing, detailed knowledge gained over decades. In fact, it can be said, a book such as this puts to shame the easy-come-easy-go advice that any number of armchair experts have foisted on us—so often they try to narrow the lens, get us to focus on this, taking place at that point, that age, whereas

42UP, as the title tells us immediately, has quite another angle of vision, the broadest imaginable: our time here as it gradually gets accumulated.

Perhaps justice is best done to this achievement of Michael Apted by regarding it as a filmed novel, now made into a book (a reversal of the usual order of things!). Like Dickens and Trollope, he has looked carefully at the world through an examination of character as it comes into being in various men and women. George Eliot, at the very end of *Middlemarch*, put this rhetorical question to her readers: "Who can quit young lives after being long in company with them, and not desire to know what befell them in their after-years?" Such a question gets answered here as maybe never before: a tenacious loyalty to those "young lives" as they enter their "after-years"! No question, as with any novel, only part of the whole story is rendered, and to be sure, truth is edited in its telling and in its presentation. But this is, again, a filmmaker's "novel" now put in print, a particular narration of certain lives, hence the persuasively affecting momentum of the pages ahead: stories that give us, in Flannery O'Connor's phrase, "the mystery and manners" of this existence as each of us lives it.

Once every decade the British magazine *Sight and Sound* asks hundreds of people to list their ten favorite films. On my most recent list I included the *U P* series. Michael Apted's continuing documentary studies the lives of a cross–section of subjects he visits every seven years, chatting with them about how things are going. These films penetrate to the central mystery of life, asking the same questions that Wim Wenders poses in *Wings of Desire*: Why am I me and why not you? Why am I here and why not there? They also strike me as an inspired, almost noble, use of the film medium. No other art form can capture so well the look in an eye, the feeling in an expression, the thoughts that go unspoken between the words. To look at these films, as I have every seven years, is to meditate on the astonishing fact that man is the animal that knows it lives in time.

"The child is father of the man," Wordsworth once wrote. That seems literally true as we look at these films. Theories about genetics and environment, nature and nurture, fall away; we realize that the seven-year-old we see at the beginning of each segment already contains most of the elements, good and bad, that flower in later life. Sometimes there are surprises; a girl who is an uptight, morose chain-smoker at twenty-one, vowing never to marry, expressing disinterest in children, blossoms in the later films into a cheerful wife and mother. And Neil, who was a visionary at fourteen, grows into a puzzled outcast at twenty-eight, before making a comeback of sorts by thirty-five. At seven, he wanted to be a bus driver, telling passengers what to look for out the windows; at thirty-five, he lives in public housing on an island off the coast of Scotland, has just been deposed as director of the village pageant, and feels things would be going better if he were still in charge. He still wants to tell the people what to look at.

Some lives seem to proceed with a certain inevitability. Tony at seven wants to be a jockey, at fourteen is a stable boy, and at twenty-one has actually ridden in the same race with the great Lester Piggott. Speculating that he might not be able to make a career as a jockey, he talks about taxi driving, and at twenty-eight he is content as a London cabby, happy with a wife and two children, talking about his annual holidays in Spain, speculating about opening a pub.

Looking at *28UP* and *35UP* in preparation for this foreword (I have not yet seen *42UP*), I noticed more than I did the first time the roles of the spouses. Although modern feminism came of age during the making of the series, it is still true here that the man essentially defines the conditions under which a couple lives, and the woman still essentially raises the children. There is much talk about cooperation and task-sharing, but in the smiles and shrugs and glances into the distance we read the rest of the message.

One subject, an Oxford graduate, found that his first job in England represented a decline in his standard of living from his undergraduate days. He took a job at the University of Wisconsin, where he can pursue his research on fusion. His wife, also an academic, came along into exile, but talks wistfully of visiting England only once every two years, and realizing that she can expect to see some of her family members perhaps only ten more times in her lifetime. Talking about raising a family, she says optimistically (in 1984) that a computer in the home may help her juggle work and domestic duties. Another wife doesn't want children because they will limit her choices; on the basis of the experience of the others in the film, she's right. Still, film makes its response by showing subjects dubious about children at twenty-one but treasuring them at twenty-eight or thirty-five.

Because all the subjects are British, there are qualities that leap out for an American viewer. One is how articulate the subjects are; from the three working-class girls in a pub to the well-born graduates of the best schools, from the taxi driver to the Cockney who moved with his wife to Australia, they're all good at self-expression. They speak with precision, and often with grace and humor. They have style. One ponders the inarticulate murkiness, self-help clichés, sports metaphors, and management truisms that clutter American speech.

It is also evident that class counts for more in Britain than in America. One woman says she believed when she was younger that there were "opportunities," but now sees that she was deceived. There is a curious way in which we sense that those in the middle are the least content; the working classes seem sure of themselves, confident in their idiom, realistic

and humorous. The fortunate also seem to have examined their options and found interesting ones. Those caught in the middle seem more trapped, unless education has released them; the nuclear physicist relaxes on the shores of Lake Mendota and talks about how American universities function as British comprehensive schools were intended to, by casting a wide net and opening up opportunities for every generation.

Watching the films again, I also became more aware of the larger role the countryside plays in British lives. Many of the subjects live in or visit the country, and are at home with gardening and the outdoors; during one interview the camera casually changes focus to show the subject's dog, in the background, capturing a rabbit.

And what about the subjects themselves? At seven they could hardly have volunteered for this project, and now they are stuck with it. For better or worse, they are held to an accounting every seven years. The series plays on British television, so that their notoriety is renewed on a regular basis; it doesn't help to grow grey or wrinkled, because the cameras keep up with them. Some of them refer to the project half—ruefully, but there have been fewer dropouts than one would imagine, and one subject came back in from the cold. Even Neil, the loner who has become the most worrisome of the subjects, comes forward. It's as if they all accept that they are part of an enterprise larger than themselves, and indeed they are. They provide the materials for a project that exploits, more fully than any other, the use of cinema as a time machine.

Looking forward to *42UP*, I wonder how Neil is doing. I wonder if anyone has developed an illness, or died. If there have been divorces. If there have been upheavals in occupation or lifestyle. I wonder how changes in society, such as the computer revolution, have affected the subjects. Having seen the subjects through the Thatcher years, I wonder how things are for them under Blair. In asking these questions about them, I am asking similar questions about myself.

One of the values of this book is its ability to provide information on the participants beyond what is in the films. The last time I spoke to Michael Apted, he noted the inevitable difficulty of covering more years every time with a film of the same length. Here the Q&A format lets us learn more about these people, whose lives are different from our own and yet shed light for us. Samuel Beckett observed that we are born astride a grave, the light gleams an instant, then it's night once more. But that instant is ours, to do with as we can. In following these journeys through life, I am reminded every seven years that although many things seem foreordained in childhood, others change. We grow, we learn, we adapt.

No doubt scholars can find fault with this series. It doesn't address the various theories of personality development that have gone in and out of fashion since the films began. As more and more years pass, the segments devoted to each subject grow more crowded. Apted is probably not penetrating to their deepest secrets, but that would not be the point. This is not an exposé but a meditation. The real work goes on in the mind of the beholder. Revisiting these now-familiar faces, seeing how they've done, I think of my own life. Curious how, at seven, I wanted to be a newspaperman (like the father of my best friend), and how today I am one. Curious about my most stubborn personality trait: I am compelled to reject the majority choice, and embrace what I see as the superior alternative. Anyone watching these films goes through a similar process of self-examination, I imagine. Why am I me and why not you? Why am I here and why not there?

EDITOR'S NOTE
by BENNETT SINGER

This book would not have been possible without the cooperation of the men and women who have been part of the UP series since its inception. Their words, gathered over thirty-five years, form the basis of this collection; while interview transcripts have been edited for clarity and condensed in light of space limitations, they are presented here in a question-and-answer format to preserve the spirit in which these conversations took place. Each of the interviewees reviewed his or her chapter, corrected errors in transcription, and answered queries; many also supplied photographs. For these contributions—and, more generally, for participants' willingness to share their personal stories with readers of this volume—I am deeply grateful. (Of the fourteen original participants in the series, three—Peter, John, and Charles—chose not to be interviewed for 42UP.)

Claire Lewis, producer of 42UP, provided invaluable assistance at every step of this project and was always available to answer questions and offer advice. Much of the inspiration for this book came from the British companion volume to 35UP, edited by Claire Lewis and Kelly Davis and published in 1991 by Network Books of London.

Elaine Collins of WCA Licensing was instrumental in making this book a reality; thanks, too, to Arabella Woods of WCA for providing expert assistance. Additional thanks go to Elvene Morris and Nula Goss of Granada Television for helping with clearances, and to Kim Horton for his guidance and support.

At The New Press, Diane Wachtell conceived of this project and lent her keen editorial eye to shaping the manuscript; it was, as always, a pleasure to work with her. Greg Carter offered tireless assistance on a wide range of editorial matters, while Greg Stevenson provided much-appreciated help in preparing the manuscript.

Finally, my gratitude goes to Michael Apted and his assistant, Jeanney Kim, for their many contributions to this book. Without their support and involvement, this companion to the 42UP film would not have come to fruition.

In addition to his work as director of the UP series, Michael Apted has earned critical acclaim for his direction of numerous feature films, including Coal Miner's Daughter, Gorky Park, Gorillas in the Mist, and Nell. Born and raised in England, Apted now lives in Los Angeles. This piece was adapted from remarks delivered at the Harvard Education Forum on December 9, 1996.

I had done a lot of theater at school and at university and wanted more than anything to make movies, but I couldn't see a way of getting to do it. At that time, 1963, the Manchester-based Granada Television was running a training course for graduates and I managed to get on it. Then after six months of sitting around watching great men and women work, I was thrown in the deep end and was given my first job—to research a film called *7UP*.

In 1964, England was the pop-cultural center of the world—the Beatles, Rolling Stones, Carnaby Street, all that stuff—and it occurred to Tim Hewat, an Australian journalist who was running *World in Action*, Granada's version of *60 Minutes*, that it might be a good time to have a hard look at England and see whether or not this social revolution was in fact having any genuine impact. Hewat's great idea was to take this look through the eyes of seven-year-old children. Were the great cultural events changing forever the class system that has permeated England for close on 800 years? Did everybody have a fair chance, or did the accident of birth bring power, wealth, and success? Were children made into winners or losers by class divisions?

So off I went with three weeks to find the children and get the film set up. We wanted fourteen, and I chose some from very rich families in posh private schools; some from poor families in state-run schools; a couple from suburban Liverpool; one from the remote Yorkshire Dales; and two from a London children's home. Then with the director, Paul Almond, we filmed their opinions on money, love, God, sex, race, school, and on one another. These were to be the politicians, managers, trade-unionists, and parents of the year 2000, so what kind of England did we have now and what could we look forward to?

It was one of those ideas that sounded okay when you talked about it, but when you actually saw it, it was remarkable. It confirmed that England was as class–driven as ever, and, because of the accident of birth, some had tremendous opportunities for wealth and achievement, while others, no less gifted, talented or intelligent, were clearly not going to have the same kind of options.

We used the Jesuit saying, "Give me the child until he is seven, and I will show you the man," as a theme, and I think the power of the project is that everybody has a different opinion about whether or not it has any truth. Some find the film depressing because they think the Jesuits were right and nothing alters what is set out at seven; others are more optimistic, for they see evidence of change, of social mobility, with people overcoming obstacles and defying the limitations of their upbringing. For my money, lives can change, but I wonder whether the personality ever does —if you're pushy and extroverted as a child, that never alters, and if you're timid and shy you always will be. But wherever you stand on the Jesuits, it's certain that you'll identify with some character or some incident in the film; it'll touch some nerve, stay in the mind, and make you reflect on your own life. That's why the UP films live on.

Our process is hardly scientific, more a complicated and sometimes bewildering array of private moments set against the cultural and social background of the times. The films are personal to me (after I researched 7UP, I took over the project and produced and direct-ed all the rest, with invaluable support from my colleague, Claire Lewis) and it's my dia-logue with people I've known a long time: some I'm close to; some I never see between the years. I don't read up on my education the-ory, my psychology, my sociology, whatever; I just ask them what I think is important about their lives. We have an agreement that if they don't want to talk about something, we won't. If they don't like stuff I've used, I will take it out, because I want to go back in seven years and ask them to do it all over again.

Making these films, you get to play God a bit and try to anticipate how things will turn out, which is not always healthy. For example, I made a big mistake with Tony. He was a tough street kid who'd had a difficult childhood and at fourteen was working at a racing stables and earning dodgy money on the side taking bets at the local greyhound track. I thought he wouldn't make it, that he'd end up in trouble, probably in and out of prison. So in 21UP, I filmed him dri-ving around the hot crime spots of London's East End, showing me the hangouts of notori-ous criminals and sites of juicy murders. It was my pathetic attempt to plan ahead and lie in wait for him. But I was wrong, because the wild-ness of his early years softened, and the energy was channeled into his marriage and children. His working-class roots became a source of strength, and by his twenties he'd begun to make something of himself. So I have learned to be careful and know my place. Tony didn't hold any grudges; he just said to me, "Michael, you can't always judge a book by its cover."

I have two big regrets about the series. As the years went by and the films matured, I regretted not choosing more middle-class peo-ple. In England, the middle class went through a tremendous change during this thirty-year period. People born in the late 1950s were sent to school to pass exams, sent to college to get a degree, and promised great jobs. But of course when they came out into the world, the roof had fallen in and there were no jobs. Mar-garet Thatcher had dismantled social services, taken money out of education, out of the arts, out of medicine. So suddenly that generation was left stranded, scrambling for jobs and hopelessly overqualified for the work that was on offer. The film lives a bit in the extremes of the social system and more of the middle ground would have been valuable.

My other regret is that of the fourteen I originally chose, only four were women. In my defense, if you were going to predict in 1964 who would be the trade-union leaders or politi-cians of the year 2000, you wouldn't have picked a woman. Who were we to know that in less than fifteen years, there would be a lady prime minister? But I've suffered for that mistake, as one of the most powerful political upheavals of my lifetime is the changing role of women in the home and workplace, the conflict between family and careers, and I missed it. I was a little bit unlucky, because the four girls that I chose all pursued the family route. They married young, three had children almost immediately, and only Lynn pursued a career and had to juggle children and work.

By now I have a gigantic amount of material. I shoot three-hour interviews and end up using five or six minutes. It's getting difficult to know how to marshal all the stuff. What's interesting is how different people emerge as important or colorful at different generations. In the very early films, Symon, a West-Indian, was the leading light. He had no father, grew up in a children's home, then was reunited with his mother, who suffered from serious nervous problems. His troubled beginnings made him enormously appealing. The lives of the three working-class girls, Jackie, Lynn, and Sue, followed a fairly predictable pattern until I got to 35UP, when they came to some sort of crossroads and things became riveting. At any given age, other people disappear into the background. Part of the skill and challenge of making documentaries is to be alive to what's happening in front of you, to be alert to what's fruitful and to what's not, so I have to let each film find its own focus and weight. In some sense it edits itself.

Also, I never know what the films are going to be about. I was surprised by the way 35UP turned out, that it dealt so much with mortality. People were losing their parents, so death was very much on their minds. It should have

been obvious, but because my technique is never to prepare them for the interview, I'm sometimes surprised by what's going on and I get caught out. This time, at forty-two, I couldn't have guessed how reflective they'd become, how willing to look back on things and evaluate what they'd done. The majority have teenage children, which brings a certain tension and uncertainty to life, summed up neatly by Lynn as she wonders if she treated her parents as badly as her children treat her.

I don't know what effect being in the film has had on them all and I ask the question in 42UP (see the epilogue for their responses). There's no visible, dramatic impact—they haven't got jobs or found partners because of the film, except in one case when a friendship developed with dramatic results. Psychologically, it must affect them, but I just plough on hoping not to do damage, always telling myself that they don't have to talk, that they're free agents and can look after themselves.

They do get notoriety and it's the worst kind of fame—without power or money. They're out in the street getting on with their lives and people stop them and say, "Aren't you that girl" or "Don't I know you" or "You're the one...," and most of them hate that. That's one of the reasons three of the originals have dropped out and why persuading the others into doing it every seven years is the hardest part of my job. I pay them to take part, and if we ever win any prize money, I give it to them, so they are financial partners. But I understand how annoying it can be to be in the film, and I thank them for their time and patience.

It might have been fascinating to talk to their children and to film their parents. There are all sort of octopus-like things you could have done. But I was very clear about keeping it focused. It was often tempting to go outside the seven-year time frame when people would say, "My God, so-and-so is getting his degree" or "You-know-who's having a crisis." I always resisted and took my chances with the seven-yearly visit, and if they were having a bad or boring time, so be it. But recently I weakened and broke my rule by sending a camera crew to Bruce and Penny's wedding, which took place prior to the scheduled filming of *42UP*. The opportunity was so seductive that I couldn't resist. However, it's best to be disciplined, because with six generations of material, it's hard enough to follow the stories without muddying the structure and running the risk of making it all hopelessly confusing.

Over thirty-five years these six films have become a kind of road map of contemporary English history and have been a personal marker for me as they've engaged my entire working life. I married, had children and moved to America, and wondered whether the choices I've made have been as preordained as some of those in *7UP*. I've brought up my own children mindful of those I've filmed who grew up burdened by so much parental ambition that their lives have gone seriously awry. You can see the charm of a seven-year-old become stress at fourteen and disappointment at twenty-one. I look at Nick, at seven, a farmer's son from Yorkshire, and then at twenty-eight, a young academic at the University of Wisconsin, in the process of relocating his family to America, much as I did, homesick for England and trying to identify and hang on to those of his roots that would give him his strength. I

watch him try to make a go of it here, with all the pain, compromise, and conflict that transplanting brings to your life.

After I had done *28UP*, I was asked to show it in America. I really didn't want to do that, because even though I was living and working here, I felt Americans wouldn't understand the film. How can you understand the English class system if you don't know, say, the difference between a public, private, or comprehensive school, or you're baffled by the complicated cultural short-hand? I didn't want to show a piece of work that was so close to me only to have it be misunderstood. But I was wrong. People did respond to it, and not only here but all over the world. And then I had an epiphany: I realized for the first time, after twenty years on the project, that I really hadn't made a political film at all. What I had seen as a significant statement about the English class system was in fact a humanistic document about the real issues of life—about growing up; about coming to terms with failure, success, disappointment; about issues of family and all the things that everybody can relate to.

I believe my greatest contribution to the whole project has been to hang in and give it continuity. I remember sitting with Mike Scott, then the Granada Controller of Programmes, in Los Angeles in 1983 and saying wasn't it about time for *28UP*, and him telling me that it would never happen because I wouldn't leave my Hollywood career and go back and do it. He couldn't have guessed the power the films have in my life and how I doubt whether I'll ever do anything as important as this again; important, for in a unique way, you get a glimpse of the drama of what makes people who they are.

TONY

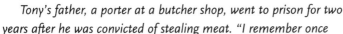

"The poverty was there," says Tony, recalling his childhood in London's East End, "but I never knew what it was. I would honestly say I had more than some other kids. You know why? Because I had adventure." Swimming in the canal at Victoria Park, playing hide-and-seek, making regular Saturday pilgrimages to the movies, climbing over walls and drainpipes—these were among Tony's early exploits. Until he was five, Tony shared a bed with his older brothers Johnny and Joey; when the family moved to a flat in Waterloo Gardens, Tony and his brothers each got their own bed—but instead of blankets, they used old coats and jackets to keep warm.

Tony's father, a porter at a butcher shop, went to prison for two years after he was convicted of stealing meat. "I remember once asking mum where he was," Tony says, "and she said he was building huts for the Germans!" Following his release from prison, Tony's dad immersed himself in gambling, with limited success. When the Walkers faced particularly hard times, Tony's mother took family items, including her iron, to the local pawnshop.

As a five-year-old, Tony earned half a crown per week by working at a neighborhood fruit shop. He attended Mowlem Street Primary School, where he was one of thirty students in his class; on Sunday, he went to bible study at Mildmay Mission. Even there, he managed to find adventure: "All the kids used to line up for orange and biscuit," he remembers, "and I'd go round twice, wearing some other kid's coat and standing on tiptoe."

7 TEACHER AT MOWLEM STREET PRIMARY SCHOOL: Would everybody please sit round now and get on with their work? I don't want to see any backs to me. Tony, do you hear as well? Get on with your work in front. Tony! Don't turn round again.

Q: **Tony, do you think it's important to fight?**
TONY: Is it important to fight? Yes! The poshies… "Oh yes, oh yes, oh yes." They're nuts. Just have to touch them, and they say, "O! O! O!"

Q: **What do you want to be when you grow up?**
TONY: I want to be a jockey when I grow up. Yeah, I want to be a jockey when I grow up!

TONY

14 At fourteen, Tony was working as a stable boy.

TONY: My dad got on to Tommy Gosling, and Mr. Gosling told me I could come here [to his racing stables at Epsom] for every school holiday and learn a bit more. Next April, I'll be leaving school and I'll work for him for good.

Q: **Did your parents encourage you to do this?**
TONY: Yes, they're pleased with everything I'm going to do. They always have wanted me to be a jockey.

Q: **Why?**
TONY: The enjoyment—just saying, "My son's a jockey."

Q: **What will you do if you don't make it as a jockey?**
TONY: Well, I don't know. If I know I couldn't be one, I'd get out of the running— I wouldn't bother.

Q: **And what do you think you would do then?**
TONY: Do a line on taxis—a taxi driver.

Q: **What do you do in the evenings?**
TONY: Go dog racing, sometimes. I go in there for something to do at night. I don't usually go out much at night—stay in and watch telly.

Q: **Have you ever been abroad?**
TONY: Austria.

Q: **What was it like?**
TONY: Not bad.

Q: **Would you like to travel?**
TONY: No.

Q: **Have you got a girlfriend?**
TONY: No.

Q: **Would you like to have a girlfriend?**
TONY: No.

Q: **How much money do you spend in a week?**
TONY: Well, my dad gives me about £2 a week, and my mum gives me about thirty shillings and my brother gives me some, and Mr. Gosling gives me £4 pocket money every week.

Q: **What do you think of rich people?**
TONY: Well, they can get what they want, can't they? They can just ask for money and they get it. They can buy what they want.

Q: **What effect do you think it has on them?**
TONY: It spoils them, doesn't it?

21

At twenty-one, Tony had given up a career as a jockey and was studying to be a taxi driver.

TONY (pointing to photograph): This is a photo-finish, when I rode at Newbury. I'm the one with the white cap and I was leading a length and a half for third place and I had a photo-finish, so I took it out of the box and kept it as a souvenir.

Q: **Do you have any other pictures of you as a jockey?**
TONY: Yeah... I've got a lot of 'em.

Q: **Tell me about them.**
TONY: That one is when I was at Windsor. That was my last ride on the old horse— a lovely old horse. I'll never forget him.

Q: **How many rides did you have?**
TONY: Only three.

Q: **Why was that?**
TONY: Well, obviously if I was good enough, I would have had more. That was the first day I ever put on my silks. That was my first ride ever.

Q: **What did it feel like?**
TONY: What did it feel like—there are no words that can explain how I felt!

That one was going into the parade ring— they're not very good, my brother I mean, at taking photos.

Q: **Describe the feeling. Go on.**
TONY: Describe? Well, I mean, Frankie Durr like, he was told to look after me. I went in there, I said, "I don't know, my first ride," and he said, "All right, don't worry—the Governor's told me to look after you." And so I was

standing there in my silks and I felt good, you know. I could see all the faces—Geoff Lewis, Frankie Durr—and I thought to myself all of a sudden, I'm in the same room getting changed! So I walk in the parade ring and all my family's there, all saying, "Go on, Tony!" and the Governor come over and says, "You've got to do this to the horse, you've got to hold him back, you do half pace, keep your hands down, keep him in the rails." And I'm going, "Yeah, yeah," and nod, nod. Then all of a sudden when he says, "Jockeys, please mount," and the bell went ding, ding, then I thought to myself, Here I was yesterday, sort of nobody, and here I am today—I'm the king, right? I felt like king for one day—well, for ten minutes.

Q: **Do you regret not making it?**
TONY: Well, I would've given my right arm at the time to become a jockey. But now, well, I wasn't good enough; it's as easy as that.

Q: **And what will you do now?**
TONY: I will be a cab driver—well, how can I fail? I've got one brother, a taxi driver, pulling me, and the other brother pushing me—I've

got to make it. I will be a cab driver, I know I will, and I want to prove any person who thinks I can't be a cab driver wrong and get that badge and put it right in their face just to tell them how wrong they can be and how underestimated I am.

Q: **Apart from learning all the London streets for the Taxi Knowledge, how do you spend your time?**
TONY: Three afternoons a week I place bets for the punters at Hackney Wick Greyhound Stadium. I go out here and I earn my money. It's my sort of living, I can say, until the time I am a cab driver. You know what I mean, the freedom's here and that is the main thing I want.

If your father gambles, he gambles. Some people drink and they can't get out of drinking; some people smoke and they can't stop smoking. But I think I'm certainly on the ground with the gambling. I know you can't win gambling, putting money on the dogs and horses, I know that—but when you put other people's money on, well you can't lose.

Q: **What do they call you here?**
TONY: I reckon a pest, or something like that, because I'm always running and sort of doing everything that I shouldn't be doing. I mean, I thought I was going to get barred one day because I used to—oh, I don't mean I make a nuisance of myself to the other patrons of the place. I mean, they wouldn't want to see a little boy nip in between their feet, running, putting a bet on here for a race, you understand? They'd say, what's he doing, is he mad? I mean, I walk up there and I order the tea. There could be eight people in front of me

and I just go, "Can I have a tea, please, tea, please"—five times—"tea, please, tea, please," and they've got to serve me to get rid of me, you understand? That's how you've got to do it, just keep on and on and on, and they go, "You're driving me mad, here you are, get rid of him." It's as easy as that.

That's the way to get on in life, just be annoyance, annoyance all the time to a person and they go, "Oh, you're driving me mad, get him away from me," and then they more or less, they give you the first option.

Q: **You're very short. Has that been much problem?**
TONY: Well, a bird said to me the other day, she said, "Ain't you small?" So I said, "But you're ugly. At least I can grow." Now what can they **say** to that? They can't say anything, can they? I looked at her tits, she was only about a thirty, I said, "Well, you're not too big either, so we're both in the same way."

Do you understand the four F's? Find 'em, feed 'em, forget 'em. For the other F, I'll let you use your own discretion. I mean, this one [girl I met], I done the three F's, but I couldn't forget her. It sounds silly, but it's the only way I could put it.

Q: **Tell me about your family. Are you fairly closely knit?**
TONY: Well, I love 'em all. There's not one I don't love more than another, other than my mum, obviously, for your mum is the root of the sort of tree. You love your mum best.

Q: **What do you like about living in the East End?**
TONY: There's nothing false, only the police [laughs]. I'm firmly placed and there's no way I

can see getting out. I wouldn't want to get out, really. It's very hard to make it in the East End. I've got my roots firmly stuck in the ground and I'd have a big hard pull to get 'em out.

Q: **Are there many villains in the East End?**
TONY: There have been in their time, I suppose. The originals were the Cray twins: they used to live here in a house they used to call Fort Barracks because it was that hard to get into, I expect.

Q: **Do you have much to do with villains?**
TONY: I can't say I have much to do—I wouldn't say I was a villain myself. I don't go thieving or do anybody any harm, frightening-wise. I think I can say that. Wherever you go there's villains; whether you mix with them or not—I mean, it's up to you.

Q: **Does it worry you—the possibility of becoming one of them?**
TONY: How can I become a villain? If it's not in me, if it's not born in me, how can I become one?

Q: **Don't you think you're going to regret not having an education?**
TONY: Where does that come into it? It does-n't come into it in my mind. Education is—it's just a thing to say, "My son is higher than him," or "My son had a better background than him." I mean, I'm as good or even bet-ter than most of them people, especially on this program. I mean, I'm one of the tail-enders, you think—the East End boy, ain't got no good education. Then all of a sudden the East End boy's got a car, a motor bike and he goes to Spain every year and whatever.

And did I work for it? No, I'm here putting bets on and you think, How does he do it? And there's a boy who's at Eton or whatever, he's studying to be a professor, he's making up things—where's the education? There's no education in this world, it's just one big rat race and you've got to kill the man next to you to get in front of him.

Q: **What do you think about trade unions and things like that?**
TONY: I don't rightly know—I don't know enough to know about it. I mean, I'm not a politician, so let them worry about what's coming for the next day. All I understand is dogs' prices, girls, Knowledge, roads, streets, squares, and mum and dad and love. That's all I understand and that's all I want to understand.

Q: **What's your ambition for the future?**
TONY: There's only one ambition, really. I want a baby son, and if I see my baby son, then I'll see my ambition fulfilled. No one knows that—only you now.

28 *At twenty-eight, Tony was working as a taxi driver in London and taking acting lessons. He had married Debbie, and the couple had two children.*
TONY: I love being a taxi driver. I like the out-door life, the independence. There's no one to govern me, to say like, "You've got to be in at a certain time."

It's surprising who you pick up. I once met Kojak; I picked him up and Warren Mitchell

[the actor who played Alf Garnett in the television comedy series *Till Death Do Us Part*]. And I said, "Hello, Warren. How are you, mate? Good to see you." So he ends up sitting there and we go to the Langham's Brasserie, you know Stratten Street, Langham's. So halfway there I said, "Listen, Warren, it wouldn't be you if you don't sort of come out with Alf. Let's see how he's going." So straight away he brought Alf Garnett to life in the back of my cab. We were on the way to Langham's, you know, and all I can hear is Alf Garnett, you know: "It's the Labour Government and you let up here." When we get there, I said, "Thanks, Warren. Terrific, mate. One eighty." So he gave me exactly one eighty. "Listen," I said, "I know you're Alf Garnett, I know you're having trouble," I said, "but you've become Warren Mitchell now... my tip... twenty-eight pence, whatever." He said, "Son," as in Alf Garnett still, "you know Alf's doing bad at the moment. I can't afford it." He walked away. He done me like a kipper.

Q: **What does it take to be a good cabbie?**
TONY: Happy-go-lucky character—and to take as much as what any other person couldn't take in a normal job, because it's a big world out there and everyone's a different character that I pick up. Their attitudes, some of them, like the city gents, the typical "Waterloo, driver, please, in five minutes." I sort of say, "Hold on, mate, I'll get my helicopter out of the boot."

Q: **Debbie, what is it that you love about him?**
DEBBIE: I like his personality. It doesn't matter who it is; he don't change for nobody.

Q: **How did you meet?**
DEBBIE: I used to work in a pub just on Friday nights. Barmaids, barmaiding, and then from there one night I went to a discotheque. He was in the pub earlier on, and afterwards we went to a discotheque and Tony was standing there and that was it. I couldn't get rid of him.

TONY: Bee round honey, you know.

DEBBIE: We've got two children. Nicky's six-and-a-half, Jodie's two-and-a-half, nearly three, and I'm having another one in March.

Q: **Who looks after them, or do you share it out?**
DEBBIE: Me, basically, yeah. He does take them out quite a lot, but telling-offs and smacks is all left to me. I have to do all that. He don't like smacking them; he don't like telling them off. Unless it's really serious, then he would.

Q: **Do you want for the kids what you had in terms of schooling and everything?**
TONY: You're talking about my childhood, five years old, upward to seven, eight, nine. I had no money, my father had no money. I had my brother's clothes for ten years, his hand-me-downs, sort of going on my arms with holes

in the sleeves. I never had any opportunities to better myself, 'cause I was a kid—I never knew no better. My dad's got ill health; he couldn't work. I'm not making a violin story out of this; I mean, that's the way it was. I'm stronger it happened that way. I'm a stronger person. I appreciate things more now. And now I'm in a position through my job to give my kids the life that I never had, like lovely clothes—I go to holidays, I go to Portugal, I go to Spain, hopefully America next year. I mean, I want everything I never had to go on my kids. To let them know the benefits of a nice life, what it's all about.

When I said [in 21UP] there's no education —yes there is an education. I made a great mistake in saying that, but I didn't mean to say there's no education as far as academically. Yes there is. The area, the environment. And education makes a person have more opportunities in this world, that's obvious.

Q: **What advantages do you think you've had over some of the other people that we've filmed?**
TONY: Academically, probably they've had more advantages over me—they've had prep schools at a very early age, you know, they've benefited by it, which, you know, it tells obviously in this film. But as far as stability and the background with their parents, they've missed out on that.

Being in the prep school, they're missing the love and the care, what every East Ender always gives their children each time they come home from work. And the parents, you know, sometimes obviously are not going to be there because they're away at prep school,

they're missing the love and affection what they're craving for. When my kids are growing up, I want to see the change in them all the time so I have my own memories of when they was a kid and how they were, you know, and what they were like.

Q: **What do you do in your spare time?**
TONY: I'm in two golf societies, and each month all the members of each society meet to play a game of golf.

Q: **And who are the guys you play with?**
TONY: They're mostly publicans or taxi drivers and others, you know. And we always have a small bet.

Q: **Do you like the whole social side of it?**
TONY: Only with my mates, because on the golf course it becomes very snooty type, you know. I mean, I understand they've got to pay £400 a year membership and they don't, you know, really want people without any etiquette to go on the golf course and ruin their so-called golf course, right. It does get a bit of a pain sometimes when they keep saying, "Excuse me, sir, are you a member?" It comes out like that. Obviously etiquette's etiquette, so you've got to conduct yourself on these type of courses.

Q: **What excites you about acting?**
TONY: I like it. I think to myself, I can do that. I sort of want to have a go at it. I mean, nothing for fame and fortune or anything like that. Big Hollywood and bright lights. It's nothing like that; it's just a sideline.

I've been a film extra now for six years and it may not go no further; I mean, I'm just having acting lessons. I was in *The Sweeney* [a police drama series] and "Churchill: The Wilderness Years" [a *Masterpiece Theatre* series]. I see the actors and I thought, it's not quite easy to act on stage, 'cause you need time and dedication and it's very hard.

Q: **How long are you going to be a cab driver? Is this what you want to do for the rest of your life?**
TONY: Well, at the moment, I'm very happy in driving a cab, but my wife and I always considered owning our own pub, so obviously I think within two or three years, once I get financially straightened out, I'm going to have a go at being a publican. And if I don't like it, say if I give it a go for a year or even six months, if I don't like being a publican, I'm in a good position to say, "Well, I'll get rid of the pub and go back to taxi driving."

Q: **So what drives you then through all these various ambitions?**
TONY: The philosophy of not keeping still. I mean, I'm a very overactive type of person. I like to feel that I don't want to keep still, 'cause life, you know, don't wait for nobody. You've got to cram it in, as much as you can, before your days are numbered. I'm an East Ender, which the attitude is "Hello, mate, all right, how are you?" type of thing, and I wouldn't want to lose that.

I've learnt through driving a cab that people are individuals, whatever they are — upper class or middle class or, as in my case, you know, East Ender. But I'm glad, you know, that I've found out the difference at an early age. So I can judge people on what they are rather than who they are.

Q: **What are the best times for you?**
TONY: Well, two, really. The best time was when the first baby was born; and the next one, obviously, Jodie. But my greatest fulfillment in life was when I rode at Kempton in the same race as Lester Piggott. I was a naive, wet-behind-the-ears apprentice and the governor told me, "You've got to ride, son, Friday. You've got to lose x amount of weight," which I did — eight pounds in four days. And I go in there and they're all there, you know, and I'm part of it. All my years from seven, all my ambitions fulfilled in one moment. When the long fellow come out and I'm in with him — like in the same room — the starters call out the register, the names. And they go like, "Piggott-draw-eight," "Walker-draw-ten," and you're there and the big man's there. Money in the whole world couldn't buy that. Proudest day of my life. My ambition fulfilled to the highest level. And I eventually finished last — tailed off, obviously, but it didn't make any difference to me. Just to be part of it, be with the man himself. Couldn't buy it. That was the proudest day of my whole life.

35 *When 35 UP was filmed, both Tony and Debbie were working as taxi drivers and living in the East End with their three children.*

TONY: The most important thing that's happened to me in the last few years was the death of my mum. It was February the 9th, exactly ten minutes past nine. Mother was having her last — well, at the time we never knew — her last breath, and she just died with me holding her hand, and it was the worst moment of my life. With respect to Debbie, she was and still is the best girl in the world. I'm sorry, but East Enders, they're all close to their mums. My mum—and I have made it clear from when we done twenty-one—I just loved her. That's why. That's what I think, isn't it.

I know the old man, he died there and then, but he walked around until September this year.

Q: When you buried him, what did you put in his coffin?

TONY: I put three cards, and I put crown-and-anchor dice, oh, and a betting slip and a pen. 'Cause that was my dad's whole life. I'm at the graveside, I'm talking to her, I've got all images running through my mind, saying like, "Tony, go downstairs and get me five weights, you know, one and a penny," and I used to go in the shop, she used to throw the cotton in a hair curler over the landing and I used to tie the cigarettes on this bit of cotton and she used to pull 'em up and you'd see her in the end. "Thanks, Tone, see you after school. Be good." And that's the way it was, and all little things like that. Mother having a drink in the pub, singing.

Q: You've had a third child since the last filming.

DEBBIE: I was expecting on *28UP*, wasn't I, when you were filming, but I lost that baby. I didn't feel that I could have any more. I really didn't want any more. But anyway, I did and I had Perri. They are naughty, very naughty. They're the naughtiest kids I know. Nicky's like, he's more placid; but Jodie's like how Tony was when he was seven. I do discipline

'em, you know, I smack 'em, I put 'em in their rooms, I take things off of them. I discipline them, I do it and he undoes it. So I'm fighting twice as hard with 'em. It makes it harder for me 'cause he's too soft with 'em.

Q: Why do you think you're too soft with them?

TONY: 'Cause I love 'em so much.

Q: Do you bring them up the way that you were brought up?

TONY: The upbringing I had I saw more dinnertimes than dinners without any question. It's never done me no harm.

DEBBIE: I wouldn't have got away with my parents what my kids get away with me.

TONY: Yeah, but in saying that, you do give 'em everything possible. All these designer clothes type of thing, the naff gear and Reebok trainers. Now my Nicky plays football and she'll say, "Oh, Nicky wants some trainers. Have you got £70?" and I'll say, "What? £70 for a pair of trainers? Hold on, there's a stall round there, same quality trainers, for £25 or something." She'll go, "£25! Oh, no." She'll say, "He can't go to school wearing that rubbish." She'll give 'em everything. Got an old bike wants a chain putting on and a few nuts tightening or whatever. "Oh, can't have that bike, get a new one."

DEBBIE: Only cause you don't put the chain and bolts on.

TONY: Oh, I'm not having that one....

DEBBIE: I think you got to work at a marriage. I think all marriages go through stages: You can't stand each other. You think, Oh God, I hate him. I wish he'd get out. I do and I'm sure he does about me.

TONY: I been in positions, you know, and it's hard to say in front of Debbie, but it's true, it's tempting—you take the bait. I go on holiday once a year with the boys type of thing, to Spain, Magalluf, and we have a golf holiday. All against Debbie's will, but it's true, I get in situations out there that, you know, life is for living. And I come back, "Oh, I know what you've been doing out there, you've been meeting all them birds," and whatever and they look at you as if to say, "I know, and I don't want to know." That's how it is.

DEBBIE: Who's to say in another ten years me and him might have split up?

TONY: Quite possible.

DEBBIE: You know. You don't know.

Q: **If you were to break up, what do you think it would be over?**
TONY: Yeah, I think it'd be the other party. It wouldn't be for the kids, 'cause the kids, they're everything. I mean, it'd break my

heart knowing that another man could come in here and bring my kids up.

Q: **Tell me about your daily routine.**
TONY: Debbie's working in the day, so she'll be on her way home by four o'clock. The kids'll be coming home for tea. Debbie'll stop the cab outside, come in and cook the dinner. Then I'll sit down with the kids 'til about seven whatever, then I'll start the cab up—'cause we work the same cab—and I'll go out to work 'til about one until it goes again.

Debbie's got a great mind. She done the Knowledge—my wife and my sister did it together—in less than two years. For a woman with three kids, the pressures, running a family, that's remarkable.

Q: **Does he do his fair share of the housework?**
DEBBIE: No, he doesn't do a thing. He doesn't even bring a cup from one room to the other. I do everything.

TONY: Sounds awful, dunnit? I'm not chauvinistic, don't get me wrong, you know, it's not a question of that. I've a very luxurious life indoors, right? And I'm not proud to say it or ashamed to say it; I'm just the way I am. I mean, I work as hard as I can outside, and when I close that door the feet go up and I feel I deserve a rest.

Q: **What's it mean to you when you see the girls on a horse?**
TONY: There are times you look at them and you see yourself in 'em all the time. When I was a kid, right, no one ever, ever showed me how to ride a horse. I had to go out and do it myself. When I see 'em riding, I'm sort of like,

"Oh, I taught 'em that," and I see 'em doing this and I show 'em in another way. Then once they learn it, I sort of like pat 'em on their bum, sort of put 'em on automatic pilot, you know, and they're on their own. But that's what life's all about, isn't it? Giving your kids all the opportunities that give 'em the benefits that you never had.

Horses were my whole life, flesh, blood, in my veins, the smell—everything.

Q: **What became of your plan to open a pub?**
TONY: We did eventually get a pub, about eighteen months after, wasn't it? And we went in partnership with my brother-in-law, and I saw the pub going in one direction, he saw it going in another one. And after about eight months or a year, wasn't it, we decided to call it a day.

I've always said there's never ever a thing in my life I've never set out to do that I've never achieved. I wanted to be a jockey; thank God, I rode in a race with Lester Piggott and I did it. I wanted to be in the film game, and I got in it —working with Steven Spielberg for two weeks on one of his films. I made it happen on my terms, and no one can say, "I helped him," and I'm a lot stronger in that respect.

Q: **But you didn't pull it off. You didn't pull being a jockey off, you haven't made it as an actor, you didn't pull off the pub.**
TONY: Well, it's better to be a Has Been than a Never Was, isn't it? My ambitions have gone out the window now 'cause I'm running a family, I'm playing a role now. That is my role in life, I feel, but in saying that, coming to the age of thirty-five, I've done everything what I

wanted to do. I've got no regrets other than not making it as a jockey; that is my only regret, but we all live on dreams sometimes. If they don't come off unlucky, you go again sometime.

42 *At Hackney Wick racing stadium.*
Q: **How does it feel to be back here?**
TONY: This was definitely the best running track in London. I look around the Wick and I can still close my eyes and I see all the voices of the book-makers, and I got visuals of me runnin' up and down the stairs, tryin' to earn a few quid runnin' all the bets.

I used to earn my money here, as you can understand, and I come here now and, I mean, it's just bare. It's like a Sunday market, would you believe! It's really a travesty what's happened here—it's two years since they stopped the basin at the Wick. I mean, it makes you feel like cryin'.

Q: **So the East End's changing, isn't it?**
TONY: Very much so, very much so. I mean, it's the way of the world. It's very cosmo-politan now, Bethnal Green in the East End. The mash shops and fish-and-chip shops are closin' down, and for me it's quite sad. I mean Hackney Wick was my hunting ground. It's where it all happened to me.

Q: **And you've moved out of the East End yourself.**
TONY: Well, we moved from Islington to Woodford in Essex and had a change of house. And it has been quite stressful up until the time we moved, and it took a long time to

settle—but in the last three years we've settled and it's been okay.

I love my East End, you know—my roots and my people are there and everything to me, and I'm quite proud to be an East Ender, but I'm glad I am out here because I have got my own kids now and I don't think the East End now is the place to bring my children up.

The kids are happier here. I mean the schools in my opinion are better. That's not a criticism for the schools in London, but that's just the fact of how I see it now. Also I am a footballer, I play golf out here, I'm a referee, a football referee, and my referee matches are out in Essex. So it is really at arm's length. But mainly, most of my East End friends have all moved out from the East End. So really now it is home from home.

Q: **You've done well, haven't you?**
TONY: Well, I've always been the East End boy trying to make good. I mean, you have aspirations, don't you, and some work out and some don't, but I put all my energies in this house and I feel it's took a lot of strain on my marriage and my wife and we are getting there slow but sure.

I've tried to succeed in life. I mean, you don't want to scrape when you have your children. You just go to a sort of elevated section, and you just try and better yourself all the time. I am not trying to keep up with the Joneses and make myself any more than what I am capable of doing. I know what I am. I am an East End boy, but the only thing is once you get your children, your energy is to them, trying to give them a better education. They

got a leg up out here from me, and that's what I like to feel I've done for them.

Q: **Why did it put strain on the marriage?**
TONY: Well, I think we overspent a colossal amount—thousands. And with my time being in the cab and the bank and everything else, you know I had to create a happy medium and my time is not in the house. My time is in the cab working to pay and I've got about another two years to go before I finally settle up.

Inside the house, with Tony and Debbie.

Q: **So what have you done in here, Debbie?**
DEBBIE: Well, when we bought it, it was very old. This was two rooms and we've knocked it completely out. Refitted a kitchen, put all new windows in, new flooring, literally everything really. This here was like a little galley kitchen and it had a wall. And it was really, really antiquated. It was like something out of the '60s, so we just really sort of tore it apart.

Q: **And how are the girls doing?**

DEBBIE: Jodie [now 16] don't like school. I do feel that she's wasted a lot of years in her secondary school. I'm not saying that it's the school's fault. Probably a lot of it is her own fault, but you know we have tried to be firm. We have tried to push her into it. She's just, I think she's a bit how Tony was. She's just not interested in school, which I feel she'll regret later on. So she's ready to leave school. She's thinkin' she wants to go to college in nursery nursing.

TONY: She loves children.

DEBBIE: And Perri, she's just started secondary school. She's a character but she's quite academic minded and hopefully she'll stay on.

TONY: An example with Perri's education. We bought her a computer last year for her Christmas present. I mean, computer—it sounds so affluent, but you know.

DEBBIE: Well, we can't work it.

TONY: And I get on the computer and I said to go up Cinemania or Windows or whatever it is. And I'm sort of typing in the keys with one finger and I say to her if I'm missing something. Perri come up here and she goes, "What do you want to see?" And I go, "I want x or y." "Yes, I'm a shorthand typist," and she's sort of eleven, you know. Could get a job tomorrow probably in a secretarial course, you know.

Q: **Do you see yourself in the girls?**
TONY: I can with the elder one. The elder one, Jodie, without question I feel is a carbon copy.

I think that if she was a boy, it would've been nearest to me, if you can imagine. But the other one, I mean, she's very giving...

Q: **So how's Jodie like you?**
TONY: Well, I'm not proud to say the fact that I'm quite selfish, I think she takes after me in that respect, and I think the frustrating thing about it is you try to tell her to go right or wrong in life and you know it's sort of they are off like rockets... and they're gone. But they don't really take things and you can't really be behind them all the time, and that's the frustrating point. But she's a free spirit and I've got to let her run at this present time. But all I hope is that she grows up very quick.

Q: **What about the other two?**
TONY: Nicky, he's quite settled now and it's nice to know. He's got his own flat now and he is living in North London. He's with a young girl and he's been with her for six years, so he's quite settled. I wanted him to go on the Knowledge and become a cabby. I bought him a bike. But he's his own man now, he's what, twenty-one himself, and I'm quite proud of the way he's turned out. I mean, he's a very respectable kid. Very respectable towards people and most of all, he's done it all on his own terms. He's also got a good job as a French polisher and he's doing quite well there and eventually, hopefully, with my help he'll own his own business.

Q: **Tell me about Perri, your baby.**
TONY: Well she's very unlike me as far as being unselfish. She takes after Debbie in that respect. She is very giving and very caring and

I am really proud of her this present time as she's going into her character. She's got a beautiful character.

Q: So does this cost a lot of money?
DEBBIE: Yes, it has cost us a lot of money to do it—yes, a lot of money.

Q: Was it worth it?
DEBBIE: I like the house and I'm quite pleased with what we've done to it, but sometimes I just think, I do sometimes ask meself, Has it all been worth it? 'Cause we had a lovely house in Islington and this has been like a lot of sweat and tears for this house. But yes, I suppose at the end of the day, it will be worth it.

Q: Why did you move?
DEBBIE: Well, that was Tony's idea, actually. He just seemed to get this bee in his bonnet. Jodie was ready to start secondary school and we didn't really like any of the girl secondary schools, and so we started lookin' out this way and the schools were better out here than in Islington. It's not done Jodie no good, 'cause she don't like school anyway.

Q: So Tony was right?
DEBBIE: Well, yeah, he was right. But as I said, with Jodie it hasn't made any difference. Nicky had left school, so the only one who might benefit is Perri. She goes to a really nice school. She is more keen to learn and more interested in school than what Jodie was, so hopefully…

Q: Did you let him make the decision or did you actually just sort of figure it out together?

TONY: You've got me—it was my decision. I mean, it took a very bad strain on our marriage for the first eighteen months.

DEBBIE: Yes. I think you know we was sort of in a dilemma anyway seven years ago—sort of "what do you do?"

Q: What dilemma?
DEBBIE: I just think everything was sort of going through a rocky stage. You know, our marriage was going through a rocky point, and it was sort of like we've got to get it together or we part company.

I wasn't very happy in 35UP, I don't think. I wasn't very happy with the way my marriage was or the way things were going between me and Tony at that time. And it could have been very easy just to part company, and then we just sort of talked about what we felt and what we wanted to do.

I think you get too used to each other and you take each other for granted, and things was gettin' borin'. There was no me and Tony —it was just like going to work, come home. He'd go to work, he'd come home.

TONY: Ships in the night.

DEBBIE: Yeah, and it was getting to us and I wasn't very happy, and after a little while we sort of talked about what we felt and what we wanted to do. You know, did we want to split up which obviously…

TONY: I mean, even now we've been to the edge of the cliff and looked over a couple of times, and we've always seemed to sort of go back and we've sort of staked a course. But I must say, I mean, it's not easy bein' married. You know, everyone thinks it is. I mean, it's quite difficult.

DEBBIE: It is difficult because you've got to work at it, and you are a selfish person.

TONY: I'll hold my hands up to that and I got really no defense on that. I mean, I do like my cake and eatin' it. And I'm not proud to say it, but then again it's the inevitable truth.

Q: **So are things better for you now?**
DEBBIE: Yes, they are better, a lot better than what they were. Still have our ups and downs and I still want to settle up and go home.

He hasn't changed. I think he's become more grown up in the last five years since he's moved out here. I think he's grown up a bit more, but he's still got to work on his selfishness, 'cause he is a very selfish person.

Q: **Have you ever thought why you are like that, why are you selfish? Have you ever thought about the roots of that?**
TONY: I don't really know. It sounds awful but it's just the way I am. I mean, my mum spoilt me as a kid rotten. We never had no materialistic things, but I mean she gave me anything I ever, ever wanted and, I mean, it's carried on from there. My mum was an easy touch type of mum. I always used to get everythin' what she could have gave me and ever since I've met Debbie I've not changed.

Q: **So you would have done it different?**
DEBBIE: Yes, I would. I don't think I should have waited on him the way I have done. And I can tell by my daughters, the girls' attitudes,

'cause they say to me, "I wouldn't do that. Let him do it 'imself." And really they are right. I've made my own rod for my own back really. I don't totally blame him for it, but I have done a lot for it meself.

Q: **Is money a big issue between the two of you?**
TONY: We work quite hard and any rewards we get, I feel we deserve 'em. And we have good lives, we have good holidays. But in saying that, my overhead to keep everything going here at this present time is astronomical and that's what puts a strain on the marriage. Hence that I'm in the cab more time than I'm indoors, and wives, you know, they always want you indoors. Unfortunately, you can't have both. Something has to sacrifice.

Q: **Are you going to get out of this financial hole?**
TONY: Yes, without question, because this is a millstone round my neck at this time. But it's nothing what two years won't achieve through hard work and determination, and I hope to see a light at the end of the tunnel—with an understanding bank manager.

Q: **And what of your ambitions now as a couple?**
TONY: To make sure the kids are healthy and happy. That is the first and foremost.

Q: **Tony, how did you celebrate your fortieth birthday?**
TONY: My wife took me to New York for a birthday present and I thought it was quite fortunate because I met the guy who does the camera on this program, George Jesse Turner, on the same flight and it was a miracle, million-to-one chance. And we went on like a James Dean pilgrimage to see where he went.

TONY

We went to the actor's studio, we went to the theaters where he acted. We went even to the house he lived, and the hotel he lived, and I went up and looked in there.

DEBBIE: And we went to Washington.

TONY: You may or may not know I am also a Kennedy fan and I recite all his speeches. And what I did, I went to Kennedy's grave and said a prayer, but I also went back to the spot where he recited his speech in 1961 on service to your country. And I recited every word, you know, off the top of me head.

Q: **Who paid for this trip?**
TONY: My wife. My wife. She worked hard and she knew it was my lifetime ambition to go to New York.

Q: **So are you both going to be cabbies for the rest of your life?**
TONY: Yes, I should imagine so. What we do, I've been doin' it now for eighteen years and you've had what, seven years?

DEBBIE: Eight.

TONY: Eight years, yes. So, I mean, you know, we are settled in our ways.

Q: **Do you think the marriage is going to make it?**
TONY: There's been a lot of hurdles put in the way from the way I've been in my time. And I make no excuses for that, but all I can say is the fact that I hope to feel—I still love her as much as I did when I first met her. I'm responsible now in the fact that I got my family and I got to make sure I stay the course for the kids. I'm with them all the way.

Q: **Do you believe that, Debbie?**
DEBBIE: I believe he still loves me and I still love him. I wouldn't stay with him for the kids, definitely wouldn't stay with each other just for the sake of the children, because I think at the end of the day it overspills anyway and it rubs off them as well. But I think if you can sort of work a bit at it, and we do work together. We both work for the same things, and I think yes, you know we've had loads of traumas in our lives and we've got through them, so this sort of little hole that we're in at the moment, you know, I don't really see that that would split us up. I think it would have to be something a bit more than that.

Q: **Like what?**
DEBBIE: Well, I might meet a rich man.

Q: **Have there been other people involved in the marriage?**
DEBBIE: Not in my part, no.

TONY: I have often gone through life with one hand tied behind my back and my character—and I've been in positions and I've found myself caught in trouble. I'm not proud at all to say this but the situations arise...

Q: **Why did you forgive him?**
DEBBIE: Because at the time I felt there was still something in the relationship. You know, there was three children involved here. And he realized that he wanted his family and he wanted his wife and we've just sort of said, "Well, you know, we'll try again." It's not been easy to try again, to get over the hurt, because I've never done it and I've never been

unfaithful and that's what I've found really hurtful, and I feel that I'm a good wife and I didn't deserve it.

TONY: Then again, never say cast the first stone. I mean it just doesn't happen with a taxi driver living in Essex. It happens with MPs, etc., etc. I mean, you know, I'm not gonna hide behind any trees and suggest I am holier than thou, which no doubt I am not. What I am suggesting is that this is what real life is all about. If I've been caught with my hand in the till, that's fair enough—I will pay the consequences.

SUZY

"I was a loner," says Suzy as she thinks back on her childhood. At seven, Suzy was attending Lady Eden's, a fashionable day school in London, and living with her father, mother, and nanny in a flat overlooking Hyde Park. "I can remember going to children's parties sometimes," she recalls, "but I don't remember having many friends in London." Though Suzy did have three half-sisters, all were at boarding school or away from home by the time she was seven. "For all intents and purposes, I was an only child," she says. "I was really brought up by nan. She was always there for me and most memories of my early childhood include her."

7

Q: **Tell me, do you have any boyfriends, Suzy?**
SUZY: Yes. He lives up in Scotland and I think he's thirteen. I'm rather lonely up there because he usually goes to school, but we used to play until about half past six when he comes home from school, and then we go in and then he goes home to do his homework.

Q: **What about after school? What do you do in your spare time?**
SUZY: Well, I go home, I go and see my mother, and I have tea and watch TV. And then I do my homework and I go and see my father.

Q: **And then what time do you go to bed?**
SUZY: Last night I didn't go to bed until seven.

Q: **Do you want to have children?**
SUZY: When I get married, I'd like to have two children.

Q: **Would you like to have a nanny to look after them, or do you want to look after them?**
SUZY: No, I want a nanny to look after them.

Q: **What are your plans for the future?**
SUZY: When I leave this school I'm down for Heathfield and Southover Manor, and then maybe I may want to go to university, but I don't know which one yet.

When she was nine, Suzy and her parents moved to Scotland. She was sent to a boarding school in Dunkeld, and later to another boarding school in Sussex, returning to her father's 4000-acre estate in Scotland for holidays.

Q: **Tell me about your house.**
SUZY: It's quite small.

Q: **What sort of things do you do?**
SUZY: I swim, play tennis, ping pong, and I might play croquet, something like that.

Q: **What about the social life?**
SUZY: It's quite fun; there's lots of things going on.

Q: **Have you got any boyfriends, Suzy?**
A: [Shakes her head.]

Q: **Which party would you vote for?**
SUZY: Conservative.

Q: **What do you want to do when you grow up?**
SUZY: I'd like to do maybe shorthand and typing or something like that.

Q: **What do you think about making this program?**
SUZY: I think it's just ridiculous. I don't think there's any point in doing it.

Q: **Why not?**
SUZY: Well, what's the point of going into people's lives and saying, "Why do you do this?" and "Why do you do that?" I don't see any point in it.

 At twenty-one, Suzy was working as a secretary in London and sharing a flat with a friend from school.

Q: **What do you think about making this program?**
SUZY: I didn't want to do it when I was fourteen. I know I was very difficult because I was very anti-doing it. I was pressurized into doing it by my parents and I hated it, and I've vowed I'd never do it now, but here I am.

Q: **What has been happening since we last saw you?**
SUZY: I left school when I was sixteen and went to Paris, then to secretarial college and got a job.

I came to London when I left school after Paris. At the moment, I could never live in the country. I'm happy down here. I mean the country is nice for four days to go for long, healthy walks, but I mean I could never live up there now.

Q: **What made you decide to leave school and go to Paris?**

SUZY: Well, I just wasn't interested in school and just wanted to get away.

Q: **Why did you choose Paris?**
SUZY: I don't know. It was my parents really.

Q: **Did you sort of feel the need to get away?**
SUZY: Well, I'd lived in London or Scotland, and I knew people who were going out to Paris and so I thought I'd go as well.

Q: **Have you traveled much?**
SUZY: I've been to Honolulu with my father about two years ago for a couple of months, which I didn't really enjoy. There's nothing much out there. There were no people my own age there, and I hated it and was glad to come home. Apart from that, I mean, I've been to France on holidays. I'm going to Australia in the summer, for about two months; otherwise I don't know where I'm going to go. I'd like to travel more.

Q: **Why?**
SUZY: Well, I don't think there's any point sitting in your own country. I mean, I'd like to see how people live on the other side of the world.

Q: **Tell me about the Australian trip.**
SUZY: Well, I'm going in July for about two months with my cousin. Her eldest sister married out there, and we're just going out to see what it's like. We're not going to work out there, as we're only going for about two months. We just feel that if we don't go now, we never will. We've got the opportunity to go now, so we're going.

Q: **How are you going to pay for it?**
SUZY: Save up and go!

Q: **What do you think about babies?**
SUZY: I'm not very children-minded at the moment. I don't know that I ever will be.

Q: **Your parents split up soon after you were fourteen. What sort of influence did that have on you?**
SUZY: Well, any child going through their parents splitting up—aged fourteen you're at a very vulnerable age and it does cut you up. You know, you get over it. There was no point in their staying together for me because it was worse—I mean the rows. It's worse. And if two people can't live together, then there's no point in making yourself, even for the sake of the children.

Q: **What's your attitude towards marriage for yourself?**
SUZY: Well, I don't know. I haven't given it a lot of thought because I'm very, very cynical about it. Then again, you get a certain

amount of faith restored in it. I've got friends and their parents are happily married, and so it does put faith back into you, but myself, I'm very cynical about it.

Q: **Why?**
SUZY: Because it kills whatever love there is. It just seems to go wrong.

Q: **What do you base that on?**
SUZY: Well, people I've seen. People around me. I've obviously not got a lot of friends of mine who are married. There's a lot of people of say twenty to thirty, they all seem to be getting divorced and can't stay together. At the moment, I just don't really believe in it.

Q: **Why do you think people can't hold marriages together?**
SUZY: I don't know. I really don't know. I don't sort of sit down and think and analyze marriage. It's not a thing I've had to come up and think about that I was going to get married. I've got no desire to at the moment. I think twenty's far too young.

Q: **What do you want most out of life?**
SUZY: To be happy, get on with life. I don't want to sit back and let it all drift past. I mean, you don't know how long you've got your life for. I mean, you could be run down by a bus tomorrow. You've got to make the most out of it while you've got it.

When you're a child, you always think how nice it will be when you grow up, but there are times when I wish I was three again.

28 *At twenty-eight, Suzy had been married for five years. She was living outside London with her husband Rupert and their two children.*

SUZY: Rupert and I were friends for about two years. And I think the nice thing is that we knew each other very well before. We knew quite a lot of the faults of each other, which I think is very important.

I suppose twenty-two is considered quite young [to get married]. I felt it was the right time. I don't see what I would have gained by waiting another three years.

Q: **What gave you that feeling?**
SUZY: I just felt I was doing the right thing, which, as you said, was extraordinary when only about eighteen months before I was very anti-it.

Q: **Do you prefer living in this small village to life in London?**
SUZY: I had seven years up in London, I suppose, and it was fantastic, but I've just had enough. It's a much slower way of life down here. I'd had enough of the rat race.

Q: **What was the biggest shock to you when you were confronted with a small baby that you had to be responsible for?**
SUZY: Panic set in, I think. That I wasn't going to be able to cope.

Q: **Would you like to have a nanny to look after the children?**
SUZY: I felt that we'd taken the decision to bring a child into the world, and I feel that I wanted to bring him up, not somebody else. I feel it's my responsibility to start him off;

whether that will make any difference to how he turns out, I don't know.

Q: **Is it everything you wanted?**

SUZY: For the moment, yes. I mean, I don't think I'll have any more for the reason that I will get pleasure out of these two, but I can't see me going on and on with sort of four or five children. I think I feel that I'd want to move on and try and do something else.

Q: **Are you planning to send Thomas and Oliver off to boarding school?**

SUZY: I went to prep school boarding when I was nine. Rupert went at eight and we both hated it. I hated my prep school. I just feel it's too young to send a child off and we both feel we'd never send Thomas and Oliver off probably maybe until they are thirteen. I think eight is much too young, so we will definitely keep them at home.

Q: **Do you still want to send them in the private sector to school?**

SUZY: I think we will, yes. But as I said not 'til they're thirteen.

Q: **Why do you choose the private sector as opposed to the state?**

SUZY: I suppose it's what we had, it's what we know.

Q: **What's happened with your parents?**

SUZY: My father died three years ago. It's very hard to describe to somebody how you just take the loss.

It's terribly hard and even now I still can't believe my father's not here. It's still sinking in, I think, even after two-and-a-half years. He was up in Scotland. It was in that very bad winter of '81 and we were literally snowed in and I couldn't get out. And it was three weeks before Thomas was born and I wasn't allowed to fly, no airline would take me, and the trains were blocked with snow, and so I couldn't get there. And I still feel guilty that I didn't try and get myself out of here and go, but, you know, when you're told you could endanger a baby's life, you have to rather sit still. The death of one of your close family is probably something you don't get over. It's a different kind of problem than anything else and it is hard to come to terms with. And it was really last year when it sunk in, that he really wasn't around anymore.

Q: **It just seems a miracle to me—when I last saw you at twenty-one, you were nervous, you were chain smoking, you were uptight. And now you seem happy. What's happened to you over this last seven years?**

SUZY: I suppose Rupert. I'll give you some credit.

RUPERT: I'm now chain smoking...

SUZY: No, I didn't know where I was going at twenty-one. I suppose I thought I was reasonably happy at twenty-one, but I had no kind of direction; no, I obviously hadn't found what I wanted. I don't think most people have at twenty-one. I was still very young.

I think both of us probably were very sheltered. It's only having been abroad that you can appreciate more, that there are people who are very different, cultures are different. But I think as I was growing up, probably I was far too sheltered.

Q: **Do you have any fears for the future for yourself?**
SUZY: No, not so much for myself at all. I feel if I was going to have fallen by the wayside I would have done it by now. I think probably I'm too staid now to do that. But maybe I'm wrong.

35 At *thirty-five, Suzy and Rupert had a third child—a daughter.*

Q: **What has changed in your life over the last seven years?**
SUZY: Very little has changed. My life is probably much the same as it was then. I've had another baby, we've moved house, and that's about all. Thomas is at a prep school now; he's a day boy now, which he enjoys. Oliver's at school and Laura's just started this week.

Q: **Tell me more about the children.**
SUZY: We didn't have a third child because we desperately wanted to have a daughter. I mean, there's no point doing that. But it was lovely when she was a girl because I feel the

boys will go off with Rupert fishing and stuff and I shall be left on my own—so it'll be nice to have a girl around the place.

Q: **This is a wonderful atmosphere to bring up children. Do you think in some way it might be too secluded and safe for them?**
SUZY: It could be. That's something that slightly frightens me, that it's a very cosseted life that they have here and they've got to hit the world at some point. I just hope that I can help them cope with it. It is the most carefree time of your life. I'm not saying it is for all children.

I hope by Rupert and I giving them a close family unit, that they'll keep their heads and won't feel that they're slightly lost like I did. Where I wasted time was in my middle teens and I think that at that stage I didn't care. I just let those years go, really; I drifted and it's too late now to look back.

Q: **Is discipline important?**
SUZY: Yes. It must be. I wouldn't want to bring up three unruly, rude children. I'd hate people to look at my children and think, Ugh, they don't want to have them for the day

because they're so badly behaved and rude. But then you know some days you can spend your whole day just shouting at them because they're behaving so badly.

Q: **Tell me about your marriage in the last seven years.**
SUZY: I think you can't just walk through marriage and think once you get married it's all going to be roses and everything forever, you know. Everybody has their rows, but we've never yet had a row that we haven't managed to sort out, and I reckon really we've got a pretty, pretty good marriage.

RUPERT: I was a partner in quite a big law firm and I resigned from that and set up my own company. I tend to specialize in refurbishing old buildings and converting them into offices.

SUZY: It was a very difficult time when Rupert was deciding to leave. He's got a lot of responsibilities with all of us and it's not easy just starting off on his own.

Q: **Do you ever worry that the roof might fall in and you'll be out of this and whatever?**
SUZY: Yes, it crosses my mind. Last year, it crossed my mind quite hard that we could lose this if things don't pick up.

Q: **Tell me about your mum.**
SUZY: She was diagnosed before Christmas as having lung cancer, but she's strong, she's tough, and hopefully she'll pull her way out of it. She's just had a horrendous operation; she's still in hospital now, in a lot of pain. You see someone in pain like that, especially someone that you love and care for, it's very hard.

Somehow I think when you're faced with it, you just find inner strength. I think you think beforehand you can't cope with it, but somehow when it's there, you just get on. Someone somehow gives you inner strength to cope with it.

42 *At forty-two, Suzy had embarked on a new endeavor: bereavement counseling.*

SUZY: I got into bereavement counseling about four years ago. About seven years ago, I picked up the paper one night and was reading an article on a young widow who'd been hugely helped coping with her grief by Cruise [an agency that provides bereavement care]. And it just rang a bell, and I thought, Yes, it's something I'd quite like to get involved with. But Laura was only about two then—no, she was younger than that. And I just thought it's not something that I'd like to get involved in now, but I'd like to later on. So when she went to school, I applied to go on one of their training courses and it just went from there.

Q: **Why do you do it?**
SUZY: It's a very raw, harrowing experience in some ways because it's dealing with very real grief. I mean, it's good. But I have lost both my parents now so I can understand some of that. You suddenly feel you are the next generation—the top line stops with you. It's a huge privilege to be allowed into people's lives to try and help them. And if what I can do helps them get through it a bit, I mean, it's good.

Q: **Does your work at Cruise help you?**

SUZY: Yes. Funny enough, we found out my mother had fairly terminal cancer when I was halfway through the course. And I did wonder whether I could carry on because it was quite difficult going to the course every week and listening to other people—what they had gone through. But in a strange way, it helped me, because I suddenly felt—Yes. I'm not the only one. And some of the anger I felt, other people had also gone through. So I came through the course and my mother died just after that, but I did find it a help doing it because I'd just felt I wasn't alone. And I think that's the whole point of bereavement counseling—that people feel very alone when they've lost someone very close to them, and a lot of people don't have someone to turn to or they don't want to turn to their family. Sometimes there's a lot of anger and bitterness against other members of the family. So it's easier to explain it to a complete stranger.

Q: **And how was it when your mum died?**

SUZY: It was very hard. I mean it's not like a death when someone is killed in a car crash or an instantaneous death. I knew for probably two or three years she was dying. But however much you know—and even in the last few months, when you know it's going to happen —it doesn't help when it actually happens. That moment when you are told that your mother has died or somebody very close to you has died—it's still a shock, however much you are prepared for it, and I feel sad about it. She was only seventy-five and you know that's not old nowadays. It's a very

strange feeling, losing your mother—it's that one very close link that you have, and it's just a very odd feeling when you lose her.

Q: **Tell me how your mum died.**

SUZY: She'd smoked, oh, for about the last fifty years of her life. I suppose it was in the late, middle sixties that it came really out that smoking was very damaging and detrimental to your health, but by that stage she said whatever damage is done, it's done. And she said, "I've smoked all my life and I'm too old to give it up now." So she went on with that knowing the dangers.

I've watched my mother die of lung cancer and it was horrible. I mean you just feel so utterly, utterly helpless. The care she was given was fantastic; I can't criticize anybody on that. They were wonderful to her. I hope she died with as little pain as possible.

Q: **Were you with her at the end?**

SUZY: Yes, but not actually right at the end. My three half-sisters, we'd all been with her all day. She was very peaceful, we'd all got there the night before and she knew us, I think. She realized we were all there, which for us was lovely that she was aware of it, we were all there for her. And the next day she'd been given a lot of painkillers and she was very drowsy. She'd slept on and off, mostly during the day, and at the end of the afternoon we all left for a bit as she was asleep, and we left her. And it was extraordinary: she died. I was staying with one of my sisters and we were driving back to her house and she died on that journey home, because when we'd got back to her house, there was a phone call to say that she'd died. And whether she didn't actually want any of us to be there when she actually died, I don't know. But it was extraordinary how we'd been with her all day and then within ten minutes of us leaving her, she died.

Q: **Were you close?**
SUZY: Yes, we'd become closer. As you'd known from the previous films, I never had a very close relationship with my parents. I didn't really know them very well, but in the last few years of her life we had become closer, and I think that's what I resent—that I lost her when I did, because I was just beginning to really build a relationship with her in the last five or six years of her life. We never had any great rows or periods apart, but I just never had that kind of very close relationship, mother/child, that some people do. I was beginning to understand more of how she was and what made her tick in the last few years of her life.

Q: **Tell me about nanny.**
SUZY: Nanny is now ninety-three and she's amazing. She has now moved into a home,

because she did become quite frail at one stage and it really wasn't safe for her to be living on her own. She was very ill at one stage, but she's come back and she's going strong and I see her when I can.

Q: **What did she mean to you, what did she do for you?**
SUZY: She was the one person who was the sort of continuity through my childhood. She was always there for me. Whether things were good or bad, nan was always there.

Q: **She brought you up?**
SUZY: She did.

Q: **How did you think it affected your life—not being close to your parents?**
SUZY: What you've never had, you never miss really. I mean, I can look around now, and I've got girlfriends who've got very close relationships with their mother and I just think, Well, that's what they had; I never had it, and I hope that the relationship I am building now with Laura will be close, but you know circumstances have changed so much. It's no good looking back. I can't change it.

Q: **Has it affected what you want for your children, the sort of life that you want to create for them?**
SUZY: Yes, I mean that's why I've chosen to stay home for the last fifteen years to bring up my children, because I wanted to be the one that did it. I still think the way England is structured at the moment—you've got to earn a huge amount of money to be able to provide good care for your children if you don't want to do it for yourself. Well, I haven't got that kind of capabilities to be able to go out and earn

enough to provide decent childcare for my children. And even if I had, I wouldn't have wanted to have done it. I want to bring my children up myself—it was just something I felt very strongly about.

Q: **And has that worked out?**
SUZY: Yes, on the whole, yes.

Q: **What have been the big rewards?**
SUZY: Just seeing them growing up into their own individual people. I mean Tom is now sixteen and he's his own man really now. He is great, you know, he's suddenly got confidence in himself now, and having been quite a shy child, he's now come out of himself and he's his own person. Which is fascinating to watch.

Oliver's his own person. He's very individual; he and I have an interesting relationship. It's a sort of love/hate relationship Oliver and I have. We don't get on all the time but we still come through most things. But it's been a hard battle for him. He's got many difficulties and life hasn't dealt too many easy cards for him and so it's a lot harder for him. Laura just seems to take life in her stride. She's very easygoing and gets on with life.

Q: **Which one is most like you?**
SUZY: I don't think I'll answer that one.

Q: **Do you see qualities of yourself in them, do you think?**
SUZY: I'm quite a determined person. They've all got a fair amount of determination. I like to strive for things. I won't give up; if I try and set myself to do something, I will try my best to carry it out. I mean they've all got some of that.

Q: **You come from a divorced background. How has that influenced the way you try and keep your life going?**
SUZY: Statistics, I think, will show that in fact if you come from a divorced home, you're more likely to end up being divorced yourself, but for me it's made me strive harder to keep my family life together and to give my kids the kind of family unit that I didn't have. Even when they move on and go off to university and things, I hope they will always want to come home for the odd weekend and know that if there's some difficult times ahead, that they can come back here to put things back together again and go back out there again.

Q: **You had a fairly positive childhood, I suppose. Are you making an effort to make their lives different from the way you grew up?**
SUZY: Yes, I hope they are a bit more streetwise than I was at their ages. I did have a privileged background, but on the other hand, I was sent away to boarding school very young, which I find very hard to cope with. I'm sure my parents did it for what they felt was the right reason. I just felt rejected. I was terribly unhappy away at boarding school, which is why I never wanted to force that onto my children. Tom has had a go at boarding for a year of his own volition, and decided to come home, which was great. Oliver did go away for five years because there was no school around here that could really help him with his learning difficulties. I think he found that difficult, although he came back every weekend and he did adjust and he coped with it actually very well. But we've got to the stage with him now where we've managed

to get him back to the school where Tom is, and he's much happier being at home.

I just don't like these long gaps of not seeing your children because I think you miss out. It's just interesting at the end of the day getting their comments of how the day's gone and what they think they have done and what they've achieved and the knocks they've had, and the good things. I just think it keeps them with a slightly more balanced life. I think when you're sent away to boarding school, you have a very limited view on life because you are so cosseted to the routine and the regimental life that you have at school, that the outside world is just not there. You don't know what's going on now. Whereas I think my kids take the knock—you know, the last seven years have been quite difficult in some ways and they get the rumbles of how Rupert and I are feeling. And if things are a bit difficult, they have to learn to adjust and fit in with life—which is what it's all about.

Q: **Was it stressful on the marriage, this business of starting a business? Did it put pressure on you?**
SUZY: Yes, yes it did and also at that time the children were quite young, and it's hard work trying to bring the three of them up and Rupert trying to run his own business as well. Yes, it wasn't easy.

RUPERT: There were very long hours involved and there still are, and I think you know when you're running your own business, it's just not a nine-to-five job. I try and have a policy that I don't bring work home with me, so it just means that you tend to work a bit later in the office to get work done.

Q: **What is it about each other that keeps you together and keeps the marriage going?**
SUZY: We just get on very well. It's very hard to actually say what it is that goes on between a couple. It's either there or it's not, and maybe we are very lucky. I mean after twenty years we still seem to have it and for me, it's what I've always wanted because I never had it as a child. It's a sort of home where I feel secure.

RUPERT: I think it's all sorts of things. We both have a sense of humor; you've got to laugh quite a lot in a marriage. I think that's terribly important. And we have some similar interests and we just get on—and I think it's worked, which is great.

Q: **Has the class system helped you or hurt you, do you think?**
SUZY: I can't say. I try not to think too much about the class system. I don't think it's hurt me in any way; I don't know. This class thing, I hate it—people are who they are for whatever reason, and I just try and accept people for what they are and like them for what qualities they have, not for where they've come from. It's the person inside, not their background. Well the point of the class system is that some people, you know, have advantages over others because of what they are born into.

Look at the royal family. They're given all that money, wealth, privilege, but look at them. What a mess! I wouldn't want to swap any of that for some of theirs. Money, wealth, position doesn't give you happiness or health or anything like that.

Q: **Do you feel that you've come to a sort of crossroads? The children are growing up and maybe what you have given your life for is now ceasing to be as important.**

SUZY: Well, from what I gather with people who have got children older than ours, I've still got a long way ahead. But yes, life is changing now. Tom will be away at university in another couple of years, and they'll all get on and make their own lives. So, yes, the mid-forties is a crossroads for people because their lives do change, and I think that's why I've got involved with Cruise, because I don't want to just suddenly find when the children have gone I've got nothing to my life. I'm not very good at sitting around doing nothing. I have to have a goal or something to try and achieve, so over the next couple of years I've really got to find myself something to do.

Q: **Are you interested in doing charity or voluntary work, or would you think about having a new career?**

SUZY: I think I'm too old to go out and get the books out. Now it's always something that I've sort of regretted, that I didn't do more. I mean, I could go back to college. I did do a psychology course, which I find very interesting, but I can't really see me going back again and really taking up books. So, yes, I'll find something that I will get involved with that will give me a purpose. Something will come up.

SYMON

"When I was born," reflects Symon, "an illegitimate child was something that was only whispered about. People really felt strongly about it in those days, but nowadays it's not a serious matter. The serious point is whether you stay with somebody or you leave them."

The son of a black father and a white mother, Symon grew up at a children's home in Middlesex, supported by charity. At the children's home—where Paul, another participant in the UP films, also lived—"everything you wanted, you just had it, and everybody was your friend. You never knew any enemies really." He did have occasional conflicts with the proctor who supervised the boys. "He was a real bastard," says Symon. "I remember one night—I forget what I actually did, but he made me clean all the shoes in the house. There was about fifty pairs of shoes; it took me about two hours or so."

7

SYMON: I had a dream when all the water was on top of me, and I just about got out, and everything flew up in the air. It all landed on my head.

Q: **Tell me, do you have any girlfriends?**
SYMON: Well, not many.

Q: **What do you think about girls?**
SYMON: Not much. I don't think much of girls.

Q: **What do you think about rich people?**
SYMON: Well, not much.

Q: **Tell me about them.**
SYMON: Well, they think they can do everything but without you doing it as well, just because they're rich and they have to have people to do all their work and stuff.

Q: **What are your plans for the future?**
SYMON: Well, before I'm old enough to get a job, I'll just walk round and see what I can find.

14

Symon stayed at the children's home until he was thirteen, when he returned to live with his mother.

Q: **How has it been to be back home with your mother?**
SYMON: They're saying, "Where's your father then, when your mum's out at work?" I just tell them I ain't got one.

Q: **What effect has that had on you?**
SYMON: Well, I don't think it's had an effect on me, because what you don't have, you don't miss, as far as I can see.

SYMON

Q: **Have you traveled much?**
SYMON: When I was at school, we used to have outings—go to Boxhill, places and such, and we used to go on mystery tours and travel round the country. We went to history museums for outings and geographical museums, science museums. I've been to Madame Tussaud's with my mum, the Planetarium.

Q: **Do you want to go abroad?**
SYMON: Yes, I'd like to go to Majorca, take a couple of weeks out there and relax myself.

Q: **Which of the political parties would you have supported in the last election?**
SYMON: I don't think I would have voted for any of them.

Q: **What are your thoughts on racial integration?**
SYMON: Everybody has got to get used to knowing colored people, and colored people in turn have got to get used to being with white people, because if either side doesn't work properly, then no side will work properly. People have just got to mix in with everybody else.

Q: **Do you feel you should be meeting a broader range of persons from different backgrounds? You don't think you are missing out?**
SYMON: If everybody had the same as everybody else, nobody would be missing anything. Rich people, they have all different things, everything they want, whereas poor people, they don't own nothing and they know they haven't got nothing, so they know they're missing something.

Q: **What are you missing?**
SYMON: A bike and a fishing rod.

I get a pound a week, and usually during the middle of the week my mum takes 10 bob back, and I save as much of the other 10 bob as possible.

Q: **Do you want to be rich?**
SYMON: No, because if you are rich, you get bored with being rich; if you are poor, you get bored with being poor. You can have too much of a good thing.

Q: **Do you believe in God?**
SYMON: When I sit down and think, I think I believe in God, but if somebody just asks me, I say no—I suppose it's just to be big.

Q: **Why do you believe in God?**
SYMON: Well, I believe in God because if somebody had to make the world, then call him what everybody else calls him—which is God.

Q: **What kind of work would you like to do?**
SYMON: I was going to be a film star, but now I'm going to be an electrical engineer. It's more to reality.

Q: **What are your plans for the future?**
SYMON: I'd just like to be like anybody else really, nothing too marvelous.

 At twenty-one, Symon had taken a job in the freezer room of a meat company near his home in Middlesex.

Q: **Symon, was it difficult leaving the children's home and living back with your mother? You're still here after eight years now.**
SYMON: Yes. Well, I found it's comfortable. You see, I can get on well with my mother sometimes. That's good, because a lot of young children can't get on with their parents at all at this time of their life, but I get on pretty well with my mum now. We did talk very well with each other, but it's sometimes not quite as mother and son, sort of more like friends.

Q: **What sort of life does your mother have?**
SYMON: It always seems hard. Yes, well, she's always been nervous. Not all the time, but she has periods of depression or deep depression, I think they call it.

Q: **What effect does that have on you, do you think?**
SYMON: It's made me very sort of protective towards her. I feel I've got to help her all the time.

Q: **At the meat company, you do jobs that I suppose are fairly routine and dull. What keeps you going?**

SYMON: Oh, it's definitely the people there. They work up a kind of team spirit there. I mean, you can think about all the work you've got to do in a morning and you just don't want to go. But once you get there, they make you feel you want to get the work done. We always say when we come out of the chiller, we don't want to go back in, but when we get back in, we get on with it, you know.

Q: **Are you a good timekeeper?**
SYMON: It depends. Usually, I try to get to work early, but I have periods of, you know, Sod it if I get there. I think the hardest thing is to get up in the morning. For me, it takes a great deal out of me.

Q: **Do you never feel you should be doing better jobs than these? Aren't you worth more than this?**
SYMON: No, I haven't really. I suppose I just like hard work. I don't know, but it never really sort of worries me. I suppose it should do, but it doesn't.

Q: **What sort of people do you admire?**

SYMON: I think I admire people with great ambition. You know, like people who've just come up from nothing and built up their life from absolutely nothing. I could say Muhammad Ali because he absolutely came from nothing. I mean, you can't agree with everything he says, but his word goes down now. He's the biggest thing in sport, he's one of the biggest things in life. People like him.

Q: **When you look at yourself, what do you think your weaknesses and strengths are?**
SYMON: I think my main weakness is I don't really take a grip on life. I always look deeply into it, but it just seems to be a hobby with me. I look at everything and I criticize it and I work everything out, but after that, I just sort of leave it.

Q: **Do you have a dream?**
SYMON: A dream? Not so much a dream, but I know that if I ever wanted to get on, I could do it. I mean, I always feel that I've got something inside me that would make me move, but I think what it is, really, is I'm just waiting for an excuse to use it. At the moment, though, I feel okay just getting on with my life, just sort of keeping up. But I know if I really wanted to, I could get on. It would only take a little spark in me to make me do it.

Q: **What happens if you don't ever find that? How will you cope?**
SYMON: I always believe there's something inside me. I always hold back. You know— everything I do. It's just sort of something to fall back on. I've always got something else to look on if anything goes wrong anywhere.

Q: **What is that something you hold back?**
SYMON: I think it's a part of my heart.

Q: **Have you been saving any money?**
SYMON: I often say I'm saving to settle down with Yvonne, but then I think to myself, I might buy a car instead.

Q: **How do you see your future as far as work goes?**
SYMON: Well, I know I can't stay at Wall's forever. I mean, it's just not me. I couldn't stay there for that long; my mind would go dead. But I think if I really wanted to, I could learn a trade even now if I really felt that I ought to get out and do something different. I could learn a trade if I wanted to.

Q: **What would you like to be doing, in say seven years?**
SYMON: Well, I couldn't really say. I haven't thought one year ahead yet. I think I'm still sort of young in my head. I don't really sort of take things seriously.

28 *At twenty-eight, Symon was living with his wife Yvonne and their five children in a council flat in London.*

Q: **What's happened since you were twenty-one?**
SYMON: Since twenty-one, I've got married, had a couple of kids. I don't think there's anybody else I could have ever married except Yvonne, because she gives me my life, really. We've been together, we have the children and everything.

Q: **And what is it with Yvonne that you fell in love with?**

SYMON: Her nature, really. She's always quiet and thoughtful—except when she's laughing.

Q: **When you decided to have the five children, did you want to have them close together?**
SYMON: Yeah, because if you separate kids, one's fifteen and one is six, and then there's such an age gap that they could never get on. They never grow up together; they won't know each other.

Q: **Why did you want to have a large family?**
SYMON: Well, I wouldn't really call it a large family.

Q: **Well, I think it is large by average standards.**
SYMON: Yeah? We just wanted five kids. We got exactly what we want—three boys and two girls.

Q: **Will you have any more?**
SYMON: No, no, it's a handful!

Q: **Do you push your kids at school?**
SYMON: No, I don't push them. I encourage them. When they come home and I come home in the evening, they tell me what they've done. If they've done anything bad, I tell them where they've gone wrong. And if they want encouragement or praise for what they've done, then I'll give it to them if they've done well.

Q: **Do you see maybe your kids are going to be smarter than you are?**
SYMON: Yeah, a couple of them already look like they're gonna be smarter.

Q: **How are you going to handle that?**
SYMON: Keep 'em on my side.

Q: **What would you like to give your children that you never had?**
SYMON: They've got everything. They've even got what I never had—a father. They've had everything.

I was at a boarding school and I liked the discipline. That gave me a kind of freedom. I encourage that with my children. They go to bed at the same time every night, and they get up round about the same time every morning. And they go to school the same time every day. It's good to have discipline and routine.

Q: **But what about in your life? Do you think there's been too much routine?**
SYMON: No, not really. Somebody else might think so, but I've enjoyed having the routine. I enjoyed knowing where I was gonna be next,

and what I had to do next. Because that sort of relieved me from responsibilities.

Q: **Tell me about work.**

SYMON: I've been there [at the meat company] about eight or nine years, something like that. There's a lot of people I know there now. When I first went there, it was getting to know people; now that I've been there so long, I know practically everybody who's in there. Now I don't think my mind could go dead, because I've got a lot to talk about every day I go to work. There's always somebody that says something smart.

I'm quite happy to stay there. It doesn't look like it's gonna close down—better the devil you know, isn't it? I'm not really interested in moving up the scale. I don't need the hassle of being a manager or whatever.

I mean, everybody's got the same start. They've got the gray matter in their head, and it depends how they use it and for what purpose. If you're just gonna be like me and take it easy through life, okay. If you're gonna be somebody who really wants to go far, well, you have to push yourself. If you don't push yourself, you won't go up.

Q: **And did you want to go far, push yourself?**

SYMON: No. I want to get through life nice and easy.

Q: **Are you envious of people who have a lot of money?**

SYMON: No. I may have been, but I can't envy them now, because I've got what I want. There's nothing that anyone can give me that's gonna make me any happier.

Q: **Do you think it's hard being a black man in English society today?**

SYMON: That depends what you want, doesn't it? If you just want to live in the society, no, it's not hard. If you want to fight the society, yes, it would be hard.

Q: **And have you ever wanted to fight the society?**

SYMON: Not really, no. There's no need for it.

Q: **Have you done much traveling?**

SYMON: I could have got a job in some foreign parts, working for a packing firm. But when it came down to it, I didn't want to move, didn't want to leave. So I've probably got a very narrow view of life, because I don't really like traveling.

Q: **Does that worry you, that you have that narrow view?**

SYMON: Worry me? You keep asking me if things worry me!

Q: **Does that concern you, then?**

SYMON: That's a different word. No, not really. It doesn't really concern me.

Q: **And what do you want for the future?**

SYMON: Watching my kids grow up, and when they grow up, maybe seeing their children grow up, as well.

Q: **Looking at some of the earlier films, it would seem that maybe you had a sad childhood. You didn't have a dad, and you didn't have a lot of material things.**

SYMON: I wouldn't really call that a sad life. It's a different life to somebody with everything, or thinks they have everything.

But it doesn't matter if you've got all the material things in the world; you're not gonna be happy anyway, because you still want the next thing down the road.

42 Symon chose not to participate in the filming of 35UP. Following his divorce from Yvonne, Symon married Viennetta. The couple has a four-year-old son.

Q: **Tell me what's happened to you since I last saw you fourteen years ago.**
SYMON: I've got older, grayer, losing my hair, I need glasses. And I have a young son, a house that I've never had before. I've actually gone up, if I dare say that. I feel I've gone up.

Q: **In what way?**
SYMON: Standard of living. I feel more outward-going in myself. More relaxed. You could go into the whole spectrum. I mean, I feel more at one with the world. Before, I would get through things, and if it was difficult, I would get past it or round it, but I wouldn't face anything head on. Now I feel more that I am ready to face things.

Q: **What happened with the other family?**
SYMON: The other family. I've still got five children. They haven't really taken the break-up of my first marriage too well. I mean, they weren't young. At the time, I think the youngest was thirteen, so they are old enough to realize what was going on and everything. They haven't taken it too well, so I've still got to get to grips with that and make them understand that Daddy is still Daddy.

Q: **Has that been hard?**
SYMON: It has for me, because I've always been the retiring type, the not-really-taking-anything-on type. But I don't really want to lose my children, any of them. I still want them to know that I am there for them.

Q: **What do you have to do to keep them there?**
SYMON: Well, it's difficult because at the moment I'm always doing these long hours. I don't want to be doing that. I want to find time that I can be here, I can be there, I can actually be there for them. But they are also growing up. I mean the youngest is fifteen, sixteen now; the oldest is twenty going on twenty-one. So it's harder now because they're actually looking out and getting their own lives together as well.

Q: **Do you miss them?**
SYMON: Yes, I do miss them all the time.

Q: **And how was it with Yvonne, the divorce and all that?**

SYMON: It wasn't easy, it wasn't easy. But it was something that, to be honest, was never really working on many levels, so I was getting to that time of life where I really knew what I wanted but I just couldn't have it. So I had to see what it was that was stopping me, and apart from myself there is also my ex-wife.

For the last five or six years that I was married, I really realized that nothing was happening and I was never going to be able to do what I wanted to do. I mean, I fell into place and worked and worked and worked and worked, and I just realized that I was never gonna be in a position to do anything for myself—you know, actually for myself rather than just for the family. Plus, just working was not enough for the family. The children did miss out because I was always at work, and so I kept thinking about this, and I realized that it wasn't just that: it was me. I didn't want to do anything else. I was just working to keep things going, and it wasn't enough. At the end of the day I wanted to be me, as well.

Q: **When did you and Viennetta meet?**

VIENNETTA: Oh, many moons ago—twenty-odd years ago.

Q: **And then what happened?**

SYMON: Drifted apart.

VIENNETTA: We met in a launderette and went out for a while. Then we just sort of drifted apart, and had our own lives. Got married. We met up again six years ago, and from the day we met up we've been inseparable.

SYMON: That's true.

Q: **Was it hard leaving the children behind?**

SYMON: Yeah, it was hard, it was, and it was made hard all the way, as well. But it was hard personally. I was really hoping that they would come with me.

VIENNETTA: We had the kids for a while. They were in my home for a while.

Q: **Why was that?**

VIENNETTA: Unfortunately, their mum wasn't too well and we had the kids in my home, but the family did not help. Maybe because I am kind of strict—they all got sort of certain rules and things didn't work out there.

Q: **Was that hard, having them here and then seeing them leave, Symon?**

SYMON: It was, because at that time I thought maybe the two families could meet and everything would be all right. We're not talking about a movie; we're talking about life. So things don't always work out that way.

Q: **Tell me about your family here.**

VIENNETTA: Well, I have an older daughter who's 17 called Miriam, and she's still at school doing her A levels. And obviously Daniel, who's four.

Q: **Was it a surprise when you had Daniel?**

VIENNETTA: Big surprise—a shock! I didn't really think I could have any more kids and along comes Symon and along comes Danny. It's nice to have two children, and I've got one of each. That's nice.

Q: **And you, Symon? Did you want another child?**

SYMON: I was surprised when Daniel came along, but now he's here, I can't see myself without him being here.

Q: **So he's a miracle.**
VIENNETTA: Yes, he was.

SYMON: Absolutely.

Q: **Does Daniel remind you of yourself when you were younger?**
SYMON: Oh, no, he's got far more energy than me. He's a little live wire—never sleeps, keeps us awake all day.

VIENNETTA: He's a bit of both of us actually. He's very bright and very quick.

SYMON: I like to know how things work, so for that, yes, he is like me.

Q: **Why did you call him Daniel?**
SYMON: It was my father's name, you know.

Q: **Do you know anything about your dad?**
SYMON: No, not really. Only that he was African and that he's not here.

Q: **Have you ever tried to find out more about him?**
SYMON: No. From when I was young, I was taught he wasn't there, so I don't want him. I mean, it hurts me that he wasn't there, you know, but at the same time, he wasn't there for me, he wasn't there for my mum, so I never really wanted to see him. That's anger inside me. Personally, I'd like to see him just for curiosity sake, but the anger that I've had for how many years is a bit overgrown by boredom. No, I just can't be bothered to look for him.

Q: **Do you think it had any effect on how you are father to your children?**
SYMON: Quite possibly, because in the young days I really did want to do everything for them. Just make sure there was everything there for them. As it happened, it hasn't worked out because I am not there now.

Q: **Tell me what's happened with your mum.**
SYMON: She died in 1990. She had cancer and she didn't survive all the stuff they was doin' to her.

Q: **So it's tough.**
SYMON: Yes, probably because there were so many things I never actually said to my mum I would have liked to say to her. It's just when you think about it afterwards, it's too late because they are not there anymore.

Q: **What sort of things?**
SYMON: You know, just "I love you" every day and "I like what you're doing" or "I don't like what you are doing"—just silly things, you know.

Q: **Tell me about where you're living now.**
VIENNETTA: I had this insurance money that I was saving since I was seventeen, and I was going to go to Jamaica to find my family. Then I met Symon, and instead of using the money to go away, we bought a house.

Q: **What is the toughest thing about life at the moment?**
SYMON: I think at the moment the toughest thing is finding time just for ourselves. I mean, I'm working full time, long hours, and on top of that we've got two children to

think about as well, and then we've got commitments to fulfill—you know, money-wise. Our time doesn't come into it. We have to fight for our own time at the moment.

Q: **So what's been happening with work since I last saw you?**
SYMON: I'm at Euston Air and I've been to a couple in between, but they keep closing down on me. I'm hoping this one stays ahead of me.

Q: **And what sort of work are you doing there?**
SYMON: Very much the same as I was doing before. And light housework.

Q: **And is that okay?**
SYMON: Yeah, for now.

Q: **Do you have any ambitions with life?**
SYMON: Well, I think I'd prefer to work in an office now. I've done all my hard work. I mean, when I was young, I used to say I'd never work in an office, all those stuffy people in a stuffy office, but I've done enough hard work to realize I've been doing the wrong job for so long now.

VIENNETTA: Symon's very good at maths. A couple of years ago, he took an exam in maths and so did my daughter. He couldn't hardly go to the lessons because of work commitments obviously, and he passed his O level, GSCE maths as they call it now, without going. It's just giving him a kick up the bum to get something in that field— 'cause he's very good.

Q: **So Viennetta, is it hard to motivate Symon, to get him going?**

VIENNETTA: Yes, sometimes. He's stubborn. But he's getting there, he's getting there. Within himself he's realizing, you know, that there is more to life, and he does work hard, and I do feel sorry for him sometimes, and he does very long hours which is no good for him, and it's cold.

Q: **Symon, what's the biggest influence Viennetta has on you?**
SYMON: I think really motivation, because before I never really pushed meself. Now I'm starting to find my way through life. I mean, before I used to take life as a joyride and I'd just sit back and where I end up, that's okay. But now I'm starting to focus and I look forward. I'm looking for retirement actually.

Q: **One of the ideas in the film is that you can see the man in the child, and if you look at the seven-year-old, you can see what's going to happen to him. Do you think in your case that's true?**
SYMON: Yes, I think that at seven you saw a shy child, not pushing themselves—and now at forty, you see the same thing.

Q: **We missed you at thirty-five.**
SYMON: Yes, well at that time I was really making my mind up. I was really feeling that I wasn't doing anything with my life, and I wanted to do things with my life, so now I've moved on that much further, and I'm starting to see, starting to understand that there is a life for me rather than just my life being part of somebody else's life all the time.

Q: **Is it tough in England for black people?**
SYMON: To be honest, I have never actually taken it on. I've had it from both sides: I've

had white people say, "You black this and that." And I've had black people telling me, "You white this and that." So I stopped thinking about color a long time ago.

Q: **What do you want most from the future, the two of you?**
SYMON: A place in the sun.

VIENNETTA: No, we just want to be happy. As I say we're great buds, great buddies, and we get on well. With every marriage, you have your good times, you have your bad times, but we survive through it, don't we, and we'll always be friends. We're just good friends really, and we love each other, I suppose, at the end of the day.

Q: **What do you love most about her, Symon?**
SYMON: I think it's her eyes. No—she looks after me. She doesn't just push me, she looks after me, you know. She will never let anything be wrong for me. She always makes sure that if I go down the road, I look all right. If I go anywhere, I look all right, you know, and I do the right thing, and it makes me feel that there is somebody out there that really, really wants me, you know.

BRUCE

Bruce spent the first years of his life in Rhodesia, where his father managed a country club and later worked as a civil servant. Upon divorcing, Bruce's father remained in Rhodesia ("He was a sort of figure in my imagination," says Bruce), while Bruce returned to England with his mother. At five, he was sent to the Melbreck School in Hampshire. "I wasn't just packed off," Bruce explains. "My mother had to work"—she was on the staff of a London magazine —"and if I'd said I didn't like it, they'd have found something else. I don't remember finding it particularly awful."

A highly competitive environment, the boarding school seated students according to rank: "Occasionally, the teacher would say, 'Right, well, I think you two better swap now. I think you're now brighter than he is,'" Bruce recalls. He adds that though the teachers were generally kindly, he was "naughty" on occasion. As a result, he was beaten a few times, he says, probably with a slipper.

7 TEACHER AT THE MELBRECK SCHOOL: Bruce, let's have the present tense of *Vasto*.

BRUCE: *Vasto, vastas, vastat, vastamus, vastatis, vastant.*

Q: **If you had lots of money, what would you do?**
BRUCE: I think that the most important thing in the world is everyone should know about God. I think we should give all…, some…, most of our money to the poor people.

Q: **Tell me, do you have any girlfriends?**
BRUCE: Well, my girlfriend is in Africa and I don't think I'll have another chance of seeing her again. There were two in Switzerland which I liked, too, in the Park Hotel.

Q: **What do you want most of all in the world?**
BRUCE: My heart's desire is to see my daddy, who is 6,000 miles away.

Q: **And what plans do you have for the future?**
BRUCE: Well, I'll go into Africa and try and teach people who are not civilized to be more or less good.

14 At fourteen, Bruce was in his second year at St. Paul's, a London boarding school for boys.

Q: **Looking back, how did you like Melbreck?**
BRUCE: I was about five when I went there, and then I suppose I was too young really to under-

stand it. I thought it was a bit severe at the time, but then I just got used to it, and didn't have sort of any impulses to do things wrong or anything like that. I just got into the track of what they said you must do and mustn't.

At St. Paul's I like the companionship, you know, with other boys, really—and you get that much more in a boarding school.

Q: **Do you meet boys here from very different social backgrounds?**
BRUCE: They don't sort of enforce being upper class and things like that at St. Paul's; they suggest that you don't have long hair and you do get it cut, and they teach you to be reasonably well mannered but not to sniff at the poorer people.

Q: **Do you watch much television?**
BRUCE: I used to watch it a lot, but now I'm not watching it so much. I think it's good because a lot of it is corrupting me a bit. For one thing, the advertisements, you know. I can recite about six tunes off, and it just seems a worthless thing to know.

Q: **Have you got any girlfriends?**
BRUCE: No, not yet. I'm sure it will come, but not yet.

Q: **Do you like to travel?**
BRUCE: Well, I ski in Switzerland, and I enjoy that immensely, and we went to France this time and I've lived in Rhodesia.

Q: **And how are you getting on with your family?**
BRUCE: I've been getting on well with my stepfather, and I like to see my father occasionally, and he does come over from Rhodesia.

Q: **Which of the political parties would you support?**
BRUCE: I don't know. None of the parties really seem to agree with me. I think if I had voted, I'd have voted Labour.

Q: **Why?**
BRUCE: I didn't agree with the Conservatives about what they were doing with the black people—you know, racial policy.

Q: **Do you want to be rich?**
BRUCE: I'd help people if I had a chance, you know, by, say, giving money to charity or sponsoring things or things like that.

Q: **When you were seven, you wanted to be a missionary. Have you had any thoughts on that?**
BRUCE: No, I don't want to be a missionary, because I just can't talk about it to people. I am interested in it myself, but I wouldn't be very good at it at all, and I wouldn't enjoy it.

Q: **Why wouldn't you be good at it?**
BRUCE: Well, I'm just not very good at it anyway, standing up in front of people and making a speech, or anything like that. I'd like to keep it private.

21

At twenty-one, Bruce was in his final year at Oxford, where he was studying mathematics.

Q: **What did you do before you came to Oxford?**

BRUCE: Well, I took nine months off between school and university and I taught at a school and worked in the Banbury sewage works for a few months.

Q: **What sort of school was it?**

BRUCE: Well, I never like admitting this, but it was a handicapped school. I mean, it seems to present me as wanting to do these things, and I suppose in a way I do get some satisfaction from doing it, but I could so easily have done something else. I mean, it's almost an accident that I ended up at a spastic school and I'm glad I did it because I enjoyed it—not for its, I suppose, slightly charitable nature of the work, but because the people I met were quite good.

Q: **Why are you afraid of presenting this image of yourself?**

BRUCE: It's possibly because—I don't know —I never want to feel too proud. It's dangerous for a start, and it's so easy and it doesn't work in a way because, all right, I can try and pretend to be humble, but that's being proud in just the same sort of way. I find it's a very difficult thing to avoid pride.

Q: **Is it possible that you might ever think of going into the church?**

BRUCE: It is possible. I've never said no definitely, but I won't be doing it after I leave the university. I mean, it's just possible in ten years' time, I suppose.

Q: **What would draw you to the church?**

BRUCE: I don't know; it wouldn't be dissatisfaction for whatever I'm doing at the moment. In a way, if whatever I was doing I was doing very successfully, then that would be a better reason for going into the church, really— or at least, if I did go into the church, it would mean I was giving up something for it. I think the wrong reasons are if you're dissatisfied with what you're doing, you know, in a general sense of doing a job badly or a failure in some sort of way.

Q: **What sort of job are you going to try for after you get your degree?**

BRUCE: Well, there was one job—I'd quite like to make maps. I mean, it's a nice sort of outdoor life. You travel around, but there are very few jobs like that going. I'm sort of qualified—a maths or science degree would do, or a geography degree—but I think I've probably missed it this time round, and perhaps I won't like making maps.

Q: **What do you see as your weaknesses?**
BRUCE: Well, it is mainly this lack of responsibility for doing the jobs given to me. People will say, "Why haven't you done this? Look, you've upset us." I was secretary of the bridge society, chess society, cricket society, Scottish dancing society and I didn't do anything for any of them. They were all very angry. And I spent last summer term in total seclusion; I saw maybe half a dozen people all term, darting across court. People would say, "I saw Bruce today" and they'd say, "No, really?" It was awful, really.

Q: **What influence did your first school have on you?**
BRUCE: Melbreck probably had a great influence on me in a way—I mean, I was absolutely shocked rigid when I went to my prep school and found that people thought of doing things wrong. I never really upset any-one or questioned authority or misbehaved in any of my later schools, which may seem an ideal sort of thing, but I think it's probably healthy to question why you have to do certain things—which I never did.

Q: **What effect has the fact that you've seen very little of your father had on you?**
BRUCE: Nothing really. It's something I regret, that I didn't get to know him better at all. We're both very bad writers—I'm probably worse than him, and personally I regret his not having established a regular correspon-dence, because I think he's an interesting man and he probably regrets it as well.

Q: **What do you think of your own upbringing? What have been the strongest influences on that?**
BRUCE: Probably not to let down my mother, because she's worked awfully hard to get me through school, and I haven't let her down yet. Then, as far as not having—my mother's divorce, I don't think that really has the effect that people imagine it to have. I mean, I always have got on well with my stepfather and with my half-sister. In that sense, I've had a family life.

Q: **Tell me, are you interested in politics at all?**
BRUCE: Not as much as I was. I am about the only Socialist in my village and I go into the pub and stand up and defend all Socialist policies. It's awfully hard work, really. I think I'm going to give that up.

Q: **So where do you stand politically now, then?**
BRUCE: Well, I'm still Socialist, but not as energetically as I was.

Q: **What do you think about the way things are being run at the moment?**
BRUCE: Well, I'm glad the Socialists are in power because the elusive thing called free-dom is rearing its head and the Conservatives are pushing it forward. I thought this argu-ment was smashed in the early years of this century, but it seems to be coming back and it really is exceptionally dangerous, because the more you try and defend freedom—I mean you allow everybody to do exactly what they like within limits—then the less you have. I mean, there's no freedom in living in a slum; I mean it's all right to say the chap can do whatever he wants, he can get a better job or anything, because that's just not the case. The more you defend freedom, the less you have it.

Q: **What fears do you have for the future?**
BRUCE: I have never suffered at all. Never been driven to despair or fear. I don't know, have any of the others?

It all springs from loving God and Christ, I suppose. You try and do that as best as possible and let that lead your actions in life.

28 *After working at an insurance company for three years, Bruce embarked on a career as a math teacher, first at a school in Bethnal Green and then at Daneford School in the East End of London—the same school that Tony attended as a boy. He was living in a local council flat within walking distance of the school.*

Q: **How did you get into teaching?**
BRUCE: I was working at an insurance company at the time and I decided to go into teaching without any experience at all, and I didn't think that they'd allow anyone to walk in off the street into a classroom.

They were crying out for maths teachers; they interviewed me. They phoned me the next day and said would I take the job. I said yes. Within five weeks I was in a classroom. They took one look at me and thought it was Christmas, I think.

Q: **What is the most enjoyable thing about teaching?**
BRUCE: Just being a part of people's advancement and learning and watching them understand more and being more confident, getting some more enjoyment and satisfaction from mathematics.

Q: **You went to a posh prep school and a major public school and to Oxford and now you're in a council flat teaching in this school in the East End of London. You don't feel any sense of disappointment?**
BRUCE: No, because what I'm trying to do at the moment and achieve is difficult. It may not sound difficult in the sense that you could sum up what I do quite simply, but behind all that it is very difficult, and I certainly find it satisfying achieving successes. There may come a time when I decide that I can't do it, and that's not necessarily weakness; that may be a strength that you realize that you can't do it as well as you would wish.

I don't know whether I said, "Right. I must do something," which is what I've been brought up to do or whatever. I don't know—I've just found something I find rewarding.

Q: **It's so different from your own education where you're teaching now. Why?**
BRUCE: General education is better for society, I think. Public schools are divisive; that's with no statement about my education. My education was academically excellent and I was very grateful for it.

I think there is a class society, and I think public schools may help its continuance.

Q: **Do you have to defend immigration to a lot of people in this area?**
BRUCE: Yes, I think you do. But those who say too many are coming in and so on, I think are really uneducated about the whole question. They should see the positive benefits that they're having in this country and see that as a result of all this immigration, they're not being denied opportunities. It's not the fault of immigrants that there is unemployment. It's part of a political party's responsibility to explain that and show people what is a more truthful way of representing the situation.

I just see the lack of opportunities for a lot of people. Obviously, unemployment is a great feature in many people's lives and many families' lives, and teaching children sometimes you wonder what's going to happen to them.

It seems to me that the leader of the country at the moment should be one of the most unpopular persons in the country. And yet she gets away with everything. She, as far as I can see, has done lots of damage and yet nobody can oppose her.

Q: **What do you remember about being seven?**
BRUCE: I can remember being happy then; I can remember also being miserable because I can remember crying. I always seemed to be beaten and I never used to understand why.

Q: **Did it give you an overdeveloped sense of authority?**
BRUCE: If you look at society in general, I've always probably been on the side of authority and, you know, it's been an education learning that authority can be bad and can be corrupt.

Q: **Does it sadden you when you meet people who don't believe in Christianity?**
BRUCE: Yes, if they dismiss it casually, if they dismiss it as just being something—Oh well, we know about that. We got a little bit of that at school and it doesn't really mean very much—then it does sadden me. Because you know, it's much, much more than that.

Q: **What is it about Christianity that is so important to you?**
BRUCE: Well, the belief in goodness and in love as being two great positive forces. And just a simple belief, like a good act is never wasted.

Q: **What are your hopes for the future?**
BRUCE: I think I would very much like to become involved in a family—my own family for a start. That's a need that I feel I ought to fulfill and would like to fulfill and would do it well.

At thirty-five, Bruce took a sabbatical and traveled to Sylhet, a town in northeast Bangladesh, for a three-month research trip.

Q: **So is this your missionary dream come true?**

BRUCE: Well, not exactly. I'm a teacher now in London, and I've had the opportunity to come here for a term. It just so happens the school I am in has great links with this part of the world, and I've come here to find out about the background of many of the boys that I teach back in London.

I'm earning my keep by teaching maths and helping the teachers here, helping them design courses of study. I'm also teaching them English. They've all got quite good English but they're practicing and improving their English,

and then I've also got the chance to learn a bit of Bangla, which is very difficult and I'm not doing very well at.

I see education as a key to it all. I mean, once your population becomes educated, it can think for itself a lot more and create wealth and create opportunities.

Q: **What do you like about Sylhet?**

BRUCE: I think mainly the people and their hospitality. A couple of weeks ago, I went on a visit to a family with a teacher from this school. They lived in a one-room flat but we were immediately invited in and we sat around having food with them and that's what hospitality means. If I was back in England and I turned up, say, at a friend's an hour before lunch with three people they'd never met, they'd say, "Well, let's go down the pub or something."

Q: **Have you encountered racism here?**

BRUCE: Everybody has the capacity to be racist, wherever you are in the world. I think it's a natural human condition to be afraid of something that's slightly different to you; I think that's the basis of it. I mean, I know academically it's defined as prejudice plus power. When you've got the power to do something about it, you can turn it into something very damaging to the person who's receiving it. I think if you recognize that as an emotional position, maybe you can use your intellect to check yourself.

Q: **Has a country like this got any future?**

BRUCE: I think it needs an awful lot of help. The amount of general poverty, I think, is growing. You see so many children working.

It used to be a rich area 200 years ago, and more people would call it the Pearl of the Bay of Bengal. It's not that now—and that's not unconnected with the British rule here. Basically, we don't care that many countries are incredibly poor; we simply don't care. I mean, we do raise money for charity and so on, which is excellent, but it's simply not good enough at the end of the day.

Q: **Is money important to you?**
BRUCE: Well, not really. I have enough to live on. I don't know whether teachers deserve more money. My gripe's never been about money; it's always been about conditions of work. I find it horrible that people care so much about money. There are many finer things in life than that. You know, people who bought the shares in the privatization issues just to make quick money, I just thought, Well, what are you about in life? Is that it? You know, I didn't want any part in that.

Q: **Do you think you made the most of your opportunities?**
BRUCE: My opportunity was to do what I wanted and what I found fulfilling. And I had a great variety because of my background. Yes, I've made the most of my opportunity because I've found something to do that I found rewarding—and that was my opportunity.

I see education as being very important, you know, which is why I'm distressed by something which I see in Bangladesh: the young kids working so hard. They need to bring the money in for their family. I'd say education is a right: the more they learn, the more choices they have in life. Life should be a rich experience.

Q: **Tell me about your father.**
BRUCE: He died about three years ago. He was seventy-two. I mean, we did drift apart because he was in Rhodesia—Zimbabwe as it now is. He did come back to England and retire, and I used to go up to Yorkshire and see him. Not as often as I should have done. I mean, I'm sure he had a fond feeling for me and I'd have liked to have returned that in some way.

Q: **Do you miss him?**
BRUCE: Well, I'd like to have been able to miss him; I'd like to have got closer to be able to miss him. I regret that chance of not getting closer at that time. You always need people to care for you, because if you disappoint yourself by acting badly in a particular way, you tend most to hurt the people who love you—and where would we be without having people to love you?

Q: **You haven't got married since we last saw you.**
BRUCE: Yes, I haven't got married or whatever, and I suppose that would've been something that I hoped would happen, you know. I suppose lots of reasons, really; I don't suppose I've met the right person.

I'm still a bit shy and awkward, still have a bit of growing up to do sometimes. I think I'm a little bit immature sometimes. I can have quite sort of teenage-like crushes on people, and I can see myself falling into it and know exactly what's happening but be sort of unable to do anything about it. I've had affairs; sometimes they've ended quite naturally with good will on both sides. Maybe I just haven't met the right person.

Q: **Well, you're getting on a bit. Aren't you worried?**
BRUCE: Well, not particularly. I'm optimistic. Who knows who I might meet tomorrow?

42 *When he was forty, Bruce married Penny, a humanities teacher at the East End school where Bruce was teaching math.*

Q: **You two met at work. When did you realize there was something romantic going on here?**
PENNY: We were doing the school production of "Annie," and Bruce was playing President Roosevelt and I was doing the make-up, and I had to put on his stage make-up. And we used to chat as I was making his hair gray, and he was telling me not to put on so much make-up this time, so I was having a lot of fun putting on more lines because he looked really old.

BRUCE: Made me look very old and sort of smearing that horrible stick stuff all over me.

Q: **So what was romantic about that, then?**
PENNY: Well, there are not many men who will let you put on their make-up. And he was very understanding and didn't complain that much about it and we just started to chat. I mean we'd been friends in the staff room for a couple of years, but that was the first time we had actually been alone, I think, together.

Q: **What do you love most about Penny?**
BRUCE: Well, I wake up in the morning and she's cuddling in my arms and I think that's really nice. She has a sort of moral integrity in her work which is also true of relationships — you know, very thoughtful, very sensitive, not casual in any way.

Q: **And Penny, what do you love most about Bruce?**
PENNY: He's the nicest person I've ever met. He's very kind, very thoughtful about other people, he's very sincere, he has great integrity, he's very trustworthy. He's just somebody you could rely on the whole time.

BRUCE: Oh, I might quote that sometime.

Q: **Is Bruce romantic?**
PENNY: He can be, yes, he can be. Sometimes romance doesn't occur to him

BRUCE: I'm getting better, because I never used to realize when she had her hair cut or anything like that and this used to annoy her, but I'm getting better. There's one point where I said, "Do you have a black skirt?" because I wanted her to wear a black skirt with something and she said, "I've been wearing black skirts for the last six weeks," and I hadn't realized. But I'm getting better, dear, aren't I?

PENNY: Um.

Q: **So you have to work on this romance, do you?**
BRUCE: Yes, it's a bit new. I bought her some new flowers on Valentine's Day, didn't I?

PENNY: Yes, yes.

Q: **What about kids?**
PENNY: Maybe. We've talked about it, haven't we?

BRUCE: Yes, I mean we'd like to have kids, you know.

PENNY: Yes, it's slightly a question of work commitments. But on the other hand, it's the fact that neither of us are getting any younger and the ages we are, we shouldn't leave it much longer if we're going to have children. But it's quite a big commitment and we both have careers that we are interested in and we like what we're doing. I think we do!

BRUCE: But it would be nice if it came along, though.

PENNY: Yes, nice if it came along. Actually, it would be much easier if we didn't have to make the decision, wouldn't it?

Q: **How is it being in the same school together?**
BRUCE: Well, it's fine. We don't come across each other much during the day. We don't sit in the same place in the staff room. We come in together sometimes, cycling, or sometimes we come in the car, and then we don't really see each other until the end of the day. And when it was announced we were getting married, the kids were immensely curious. You can imagine: two teachers going out together! The gossip was quite immense. But they were very friendly.

Q: **Did they make fun of the two of you?**
BRUCE: There have been some comments which have gone a bit too far, but that has died down and they accept us as a couple.

Q: **Did they celebrate at the school where you got married?**
BRUCE: Well, one of the other teachers said we've got to do something, so she organized an assembly in the lower school where we sang together: "I want to be the only one to hold you"—the song of last summer, which the kids rioted at, absolutely rioted.

Q: **Tell me more about your school.**
BRUCE: It's the Bishop Challenor Roman Catholic girls' school in the East End of London. It's about 1,000 girls, eleven to eighteen, with some boys in the sixth form, and I've been there about five years. I was at the old boys' school and had a chance to be head of the maths faculty and to teach A level, as well. So it was a promotional step. This is my third school now in fifteen years of teaching, sixteen years of teaching—all in the East End, and I have now taken mixed, boys and girls. And I was sorry to leave, in some ways, the boys and working more closely with the Bangladeshi community, but this is another opportunity to work with the older community in the East End—the cockney community, the West African and West Indian, the mix of kids that we have here.

Q: **What ambitions do you have now for teaching?**
BRUCE: Well, if you are promoted any more, you tend to be out of the classroom more, so I don't think I will be seeking a Deputy Heads

job or anything like that. I mean I may become a senior teacher at some point in the future—five years or so is possible. But I don't really have aspirations to become a Deputy Head and a Head teacher.

Q: **It seems like hard work to me, noisy work. What attracts you to teaching?**
BRUCE: If you see them develop as people, and in your subject area they get a grade that enables them to go on to greater choices in life and at the next stage of higher education —and if you've been part of that—that's rewarding. It is a long, hard slog, though. I mean it's not as if you get those flashes of rewards very frequently; you get them as you look over the year maybe once or twice. But that makes it worthwhile. And it's paid employment, just like most other jobs.

Q: **Do you not feel like packing it in?**
BRUCE: Well, sometimes it can get hard. To teach for 40 years is a long slog. I don't know how sort of dried out I'd be by then. I can see myself not having as much enthusiasm as I had ten years ago, but I'm still trying to do a good job and putting energy into the curriculum and helping girls to develop.

Q: **So you are losing a bit of that passion?**
BRUCE: I think so. I just don't think you can keep up that level of intensity for so long. That doesn't mean to say that I am casual or whatever. It's just that I think you get to a level where you can only put so much in without becoming completely drained or just going straight to bed, falling asleep when you get home. Quite a few teachers do leave their careers. Very few make it through to the full retirement age as a teacher.

Q: **And you don't think you will?**
BRUCE: Probably not, I probably won't be one of those very few—no.

Q: **Why do you stay in the state system?**
BRUCE: Well, I strongly believe in education as being a route to opening up all sorts of opportunities. Whatever your background, if you are well-educated, almost anything is open to you. I mean, if you've had a very advantaged background, then that will help you, obviously, but education is another way through. If you work hard at school, then all doors open up.

I am hoping to be part of a process which enables opportunity for everybody—not just people who can afford a public school education.

Q: **I suppose technically you are middle-aged now?**
BRUCE: Yes, you know that creeps up on me. I noticed the physical deterioration which is quite acute sometimes. I think it was last year, we had cricket nets before the season starts, so I jumped on my bike, grabbed a bagel from the bakery because I hadn't eaten. I was eating it as I was going along, cycled over to Lord's, played nets, went to the pub, had a couple of pints, cycling back. By this time it is about 11:30 and I'm halfway back to Hackney and I can't do this anymore. I mean when I was twenty it had been absolutely no problem, but I just got home and I thought, That's it! I can't operate like that anymore. I can't cycle and do two hours of nets and cycle.

Q: **And how do you feel about that?**

BRUCE: Well, it's all gone, that lightness, that youth. It's just gone. And also if you saw me running around the cricket field now after a ball, it's just comical. It's just a lumbering old man, you know. No flowing swoop and hurling in at the ball.

Q: **Can't you do something about that?**
BRUCE: I do a bit of exercise, but I think that's it. We all have to put up with a deterioration of powers.

Q: **Is religion still an important part of your life?**
BRUCE: Yes, in the sense that I carry on going to a local church, which is where I was married. As I grow older, I recognize the strength and qualities of other religions. No religion claims truth in a way. It just might help us to become better people and I hope to think that it makes me a better person, and so I listen to the scriptures and listen to people.

Q: **Is money a big issue in the family?**
BRUCE: Not really, no. I think that because my parents, they weren't wealthy actually but my uncle helped look after me and so on, but I've never worried about money. I've never known other people to worry about money so I've kind of adopted that in a way. We seem to live comfortably so that's not a worry—for which I am very grateful, you know.

Q: **Were you surprised that you got married?**
BRUCE: I suppose so, because I was forty. It was sort of a mature age to get married. I mean, some people may get married too young—I don't know. I think some people were surprised. They thought I was the bachelor type—too set in my ways. But they approve of Penny so far.

Sometimes I try and sneak a kiss from her in the school, you know, accost her somewhere, and she kind of goes, "Get away! Get away from me! Get away from me!" like this. Don't you, dear?

PENNY: Yes. Anything like that on school premises and I fight him off.

Q: **So Bruce, what's annoying about Penny then?**
BRUCE: Well, I normally have a shower before I go to bed and I don't dry very well, because I'm not really bothered with that kind of stuff. And she doesn't like that, when I get into bed all damp from the shower.

PENNY: Wet. Wet is a better word—not damp. Wet.

BRUCE: Well, I dry myself off on you, dear. And she doesn't think she's a towel—that's annoying. What else? Apart from that, she's perfect.

"When I was on my own, I was always reading," recalls Lynn. "I grew up on Enid Blyton's school stories—I just couldn't get enough of those." When she wasn't on her own, Lynn often spent time with Jackie and Susan, classmates at the Susan Lawrence School and fellow participants in the UP series. "When Jackie came over, we'd play dressing-up games or use orange boxes as pretend dolls' houses. And I can remember many a time my mum coming in and telling us not to jump on the beds."

Lynn and her sister Pat, eight years her senior, shared a room in the family's two-bedroom flat in the East End. "Dad was working as a coalman, and I remember him coming home covered in black dust. Mum wasn't working at the time." What, then, prompted Lynn to declare at seven that she intended to work at Woolworth's? "My sister had just started a part-time job in Woolworth's. We all want to do what our big sisters do."

7

Q: **What would you do if you had lots of money?**
LYNN: If I had lots of money, I'd help the poor.

Q: **Would you like to have children?**
LYNN: If I could, I'd have two girls and two boys.

Q: **And what are your plans for the future?**
LYNN: I'm going to work in Woolworth's.

14

Lynn, Jackie, and Sue all had the choice of going to a comprehensive or a grammar school. Lynn was the only one of the three to select grammar school.

Q: **Why did you choose the grammar school over the comprehensive school?**
LYNN: This is my first choice and this is where I turned up, even though some of my friends are going to the other school.

Grammar school is fantastic. Of course, we've all got our opinions. Because in a grammar school, I don't think you find many girls that really want to do metal work or woodwork.

Q: **Have you ever been abroad?**
LYNN: No.

Q: **Which political party do you support?**
LYNN: Labour.

Q: **Who do you think is to blame for the strikes, the workers or the management?**
LYNN: I'm not commenting, because mum's been out on strike. If they want the money, why shouldn't they strike for it?

Q: **What do you think of rich people?**
LYNN: They're just the same as us, really. Somewhere in the family, there must be someone who must have worked for it.

21 At twenty-one, Lynn had married Russ, whom she met at school. Russ and Lynn were both working for the Tower Hamlets Library Service and living in the East End.

Q: **Tell me about your work.**
LYNN: When I left school, I got to be a librarian and assistant to the young people's office, which is where we are now, and I've been here since August last year. I personally visit eight schools with the van where they've not got position to get them to a local library for class visits. I love working with children. You might remember on the last one I wanted to teach, but I didn't get to that, and seeing it as it is today, I'm glad I didn't. I think it takes a lot more patience than I've actually got—I'm much more at home here. Teaching children the beauty of books and watching their faces as books unfold to them is just fantastic.

I definitely make a point of reading all my new books I get in. It's quite funny—I take loads of books home. When people come, they say, "Whose are those kids' books on the table?" "Well, they're mine." "Oh." And they sort of shut up.

Q: **Did you meet enough men before you decided who you were going to marry?**
LYNN: I've been married a year and a couple of months. I do think, Christ, what have I done? And I'm being honest about it, and

Russ thinks the same. You think at times, Christ, what have I done?

Q: **What was the wedding like?**
LYNN: Our wedding? A laugh. I wanted a white wedding with all the trimmings; Russ would have been satisfied with very little. But seeing as we were going into it as a full thing, we went into it. I had an all-white wedding—all white. We were both in white and my bridesmaid was in white.

Q: **Comparing yourself with Suzy, who stands at the other end of the social scale, do you think you've had the same opportunities?**
LYNN: I've had the opportunities in life that I've wanted. I'd say I've had more opportunities than Suzy in a different aspect of what she had, but in my life I've been able to do more or less what I wanted to do. I'm not going to say on film what I feel for her, but I think she's been so conditioned to what she should do and what she shouldn't do.

Q: **Do you ever get depressed by money problems?**
LYNN: No, why? Why should you, if you can manage on what you've got?

28 At twenty-eight, Lynn had two daughters: Emma, who was three, and Sarah, who had just been born. Lynn was on maternity leave from her library job, and Russ was working as a postman.

Q: **Tell me about your marriage.**
LYNN: It is a partnership, marriage. We married young, but because we wanted to go out and have fun together and grow together.

Q: **What are your ambitions for work?**
LYNN: I've got no seething ambition to go out and conquer the world. To work with children of that age, you've got to love them, and I love children.

Q: **Why is it that you, Jackie, and Sue haven't changed so much, do you think?**
LYNN: We've all had a stable background with stable relationships all the way through.

35 At thirty-five, Lynn continued her work at the mobile library while serving on the governing bodies of two schools.

Q: **Tell me about your life with Russ and the children.**
LYNN: I'm very much geared to the family unit. We do things together all the time. I mean, there are times when Russ and I obviously would like to leave it all behind and go out, just the two of us. Now the girls are getting older, we've actually started taking them with us. I'll say, "Oh, we haven't done very much," but when you look back, we have. It might only just

be playing games or going swimming or going for a walk, but we're doing it together.

Q: **Tell me about your mum.**
LYNN: She just sat down on the settee and she died. Just like that. And we were up in Norfolk with my in-laws at the time. And so all we got was a phone call from Dad to say that Mum had died.

Q: **And how did you deal with it?**
LYNN: I'm still dealing with it now. But then although she's not with us in body, she's still with us in spirit. She was a great friend to me as well as a mum, probably the best friend I'll ever have. And as you see, it still makes me very emotional now—it's only two years.

To some, it probably seems, Oh, it's a long time, but it's not very long.

Q: **What are your thoughts on the political changes that have come about in England over the past decade?**
LYNN: The last ten years of government have actually in my opinion brought this country much, much further downhill. We have lost an awful lot of our National Health Service, an awful lot of our education system. I'm on the governing body of two schools and I want the best for those kids that the system can provide. And if the system's not good enough, then we better the system.

Q: **I understand that you started having blackouts a year ago. What did the doctors say?**
LYNN: They stuck all these tubes up inside me and discovered that I'd got these veins here [points to her head] that shouldn't be there.

Q: **In your brain?**
LYNN: Yes.

Q: **And what can they do about it?**
LYNN: Not a lot at the moment. They're investigating other treatments, but the surgeon said that he doesn't want to operate at the moment because it's too near the optic nerve, and there's an eighty percent chance of hitting the optic nerve.

Q: **So is it frightening to know that you have this condition?**
LYNN: It was for about a week, but it got itself into its own place within my system, amongst my rungs of priorities, and I overcame the fear of it. Now it doesn't worry me at all.

Q: Tell me what's happened with you since we last talked on film seven years ago.

LYNN: The biggest area of my life that's changed since we last talked is that I lost my dad—literally just after *35UP*, he died. As you know, he wasn't well while we were filming. We hadn't realized we were going to lose him quite as quick, but it was peaceful in the end. But seven years ago and it's not easy to talk about now. It was only two years prior to that I lost Mum, and it's a spit in the ocean. It's no time at all.

Q: It's hard being orphaned, isn't it?

LYNN: Yes. I don't feel orphaned. I did at first; I felt distraught. Absolutely distraught. But fortunately, Russ's mum and dad are still alive, and we have always been close. And they said then, "Well, we are all you've got now," and

fortunately they are there for me and Russ.

It's strange—the two people that were there for you for thirty-five years are suddenly not there anymore. The people that knew the most things about you—literally, I mean memories back to childhood. Many is the time I want to pick up the phone and phone Mum because something's happened with the girls. I say Mum but I mean both of them.

Q: Has not having them around changed the way you live?

LYNN: Yes. They both looked after the girls while I worked. After Mum died, the first thing Dad said was, "That's my job now." And of course suddenly we had neither of them. So we did a rethink. Fortunately, by then my girls were older. They weren't babies anymore, but they were still both at primary school.

Q: What's happened to you in the last seven years of work?

LYNN: For many years, we ran a library service to schools. Unfortunately, we lost that four years ago with cutbacks in the service. Children's services have had so many cutbacks overall—not just here, but through the country. But hopefully that's turned. I hope we have got to the bottom and it's now going to rise again, as it is perceived that libraries do play an important part in the education of children.

The previous Liberal group had actually decentralized library services: the whole system had gone into neighborhoods, mini-neighborhoods within Tower Hamlets. And Labour put it back into central units. They based me here to build up the service. They hadn't had a children's librarian here for nine years.

I do regular class visits with twenty-two classes a fortnight coming into the library. And within that, we do either a storytelling session or library skills with groups. We go out to schools to be involved in book weeks; that can vary with just talks to classes or displays, what have you. And we go out and do local history talks, whatever we're asked to do. This last term, we have been working more and more with secondary schools, which is something fairly new. We are monitoring at the moment to see how that is actually working—whether or not they continue as regular users.

Q: **Is your job secure?**

LYNN: Is any job secure nowadays? We seem to ride from one year to the next, but hopefully each year we survive.

Q: **Can you ever see yourself not working?**

LYNN: No. I like the excitement, I like the push of filling my life. It's stimulating.

Q: **What's the main attraction of it?**

LYNN: Every day is different. Working with children and seeing that books mean something to them—seeing it open up and actually helping them to see literacy.

Q: **I've been watching you with the children and I wonder, are you a frustrated teacher, do you think?**

LYNN: No. I get the best of both worlds. I have the teaching, but I'm not teaching the whole time. I mean, I still have to plan talks, and I still have to go and deliver them, but I have more flexibility and I'm not tied to a specific subject.

Q: **And what are your main areas of responsibility as chairman of a school board of governors?**

LYNN: We work as a team. Very much as a team. Part of my role as a governor is being very close to the school and not only knowing the staff but the children as well, because the children are what we are there for. To provide the best education that we possibly can for them. And it can only be done by taking on board new ideas, dumping old ones, and making sure that the children achieve to the best of their potential.

Q: **Why do you do this? Why do you take on this kind of responsibility?**

LYNN: In the hope that somewhere down the line I can actually be of some help. To see that the potential of the children that I deal with is actually reached.

Q: **How do you manage to keep a career going while bringing up a family?**

LYNN: I think we have got a very stable base. We all work together at it. I'm there in the morning; I take the girls to school. Russ is there when they come in from school. Russ cooks during the week, I cook at weekends. It's not as if I'm going belting home because I've got to go and cook a meal for everybody. I know that when I get home it's gonna be done. There are times I go home, I'm absolutely shattered, and I go to sleep. But family come first. I will move heaven and earth to be there for them. We've always had a very good partnership. I couldn't do it without him. I couldn't do it without their cooperation, either.

Q: **Do you think it's hard on women generally holding a career down?**

LYNN: I think it comes down to the individual. It has to be an individual choice that only you can personally make, because it's not right for some, it's right for others. I would have pulled my hair out being indoors all day and every day with the kids going out. We have quality time. I come out from home and I work with children, but it's different. They are not mine and I can go home and leave that. I go home to mine.

Q: **Has your having a job put pressure on the marriage or on the relationship with the girls?**

LYNN: No, because I've always done it. I've always had a job. They don't know Mum any different. Yes, obviously I think there are times that they wish that I was there all the time, but you go through stages. I mean, now they're old enough.

The girls do their own thing—not so much Sarah but certainly Emma. She gets herself involved in family life up to a point. What she wants to be involved in, she'll be involved in. But she's got her own life now, and she's building that life and she's making her own decisions. That's what gets me: the hardest thing as a parent is to let go. You bring them up with giving them enough confidence in themselves to do it, and then when they do it, you don't like it.

Q: **Looking at your girls, what does that make you think about your own childhood?**

LYNN: God, did we really put our parents through that? I've got two teenage girls wanting to do their own thing, and I'd love to be able to talk to my mum and dad and say,

"Really, did I really put you through that?" I remember some of it, and God, yes, I must have, but until you go through it with your own, you never, ever realize that that's what hell you put your parents through. Because here we are as parents, only wanting the best for our children, but they think they know it all.

Q: **Were you volatile as a child, then?**

LYNN: Yeah, certainly in my teens. I mean, with the girls in their teens now, I've looked back and thought Emma is very much like I was. Very independent. Sarah's much more placid.

Q: **Are your girls growing up in the same sort of society that you grew up in?**

LYNN: Well, no. We've had so many developments in information technology and things that I think they have got more opportunity, to be honest, because of the way things are spreading. At seven we didn't even have television on all day. Now we can send e-mail to America at the flick of a button and get something back immediately. Hopefully, they'll take advantage of it.

Q: **Would you ever come back and live in the East End?**

LYNN: No. It's altered. We like open space and there's not very much left. And to be perfectly honest, the East End is too expensive.

Q: **It's now a multiracial society. What is your feeling about that?**

LYNN: It's different, but children—everybody's the same, whatever their race, whatever their color. It's different cultures mixing together, and that's interesting in seeing that, in actually watching the transition. I mean, ten years ago, I had to learn Bengali because the children were arriving here straight from Bangladesh with not a word of English. But I can see an erosion of their culture happening to them. Hopefully, it will come through and they will see it as a good thing that's happening. But I don't know. I can't remember the last time I saw a Bengali child who couldn't speak any English. We have a lot now who actually can't read Bengali.

Q: **Is that one of the challenges of your job — a multiracial society?**
LYNN: Yes, I mean, we are going through it at the moment. It's the run up to Ramadan, and a lot of these children are fasting. We are actually getting some in during their lunch hour — they come into the library, they come over to see us.

Q: **Do you remember when you fell in love with books?**
LYNN: Oh, God, I don't know. I used to read under the covers with a torch, so very young. I was always reading.

Q: **You talk a lot about your marriage. Why is it so successful?**
LYNN: I think if we could answer that, everybody's would be successful. I don't know, I mean we work at it. It's give and take. We are there together and we love each other and we've never stopped.

Q: **What's the give and take you talk about?**
LYNN: We share, we give, we take, we talk, we organize. If I'm perhaps not keen on one thing, maybe I can talk him round, or I'm not that bothered by it and vice versa.

Q: **When you were thirty-five, you were worried about your health. What's happened about that?**
LYNN: I've still got this malformation and it'll always be there. Obviously, I have had it from birth, but it doesn't worry me — that's all.

Q: **Do you have much trouble with that?**
LYNN: None at all.

Q: **What's the prognosis with that?**
LYNN: It's unlikely to do anything. There is a one percent chance that it could hemorrhage. I've got more chance being knocked down crossing the street, and in that perspective, I don't worry about it at all. Don't even think about it.

Q: **What's the toughest thing about life at the moment?**
LYNN: There's nothing tough at the moment.

Q: **Have you been lucky?**
LYNN: Yes.

Q: **Why?**
LYNN: It's worked for me. I was lucky that Russ and I got married. We had time to establish a relationship before we had the children, and we had them when we decided. We planned that they were going to come along at the right time for us. And we see it going through and they're moving on, and we will still have a life of our own. I'm Russ's wife, I'm Emma and Sarah's mum — but overall I'm me, and I've still managed to maintain that.

"I don't remember having much of an opinion about living on a farm," explains Nick. "The farm was just something that was there." The eldest of three brothers, Nick grew up in the Yorkshire Dales, in the north of England. The family lived in a ramshackle farmhouse with a sink carved out of granite and crumbly limestone walls. "Some of the walls crumbled rather more than you might like," Nick recalls. "My bedroom had a hole at one point that went all the way through to the outside."

Though sheep and cows were plentiful in Nick's village, children were scarce, and Nick spent much of his childhood in the company of adults. An avid reader, he attended a one-room school in Arncliffe. "The teachers were wonderful—one woman keeping the whole mob of us of all different ages together." The hardest thing he had to learn was long division, Nick says. "And I never liked playtime. I wished the teachers wouldn't send us out because all we did was fight."

7

Q: **What do you want to be when you grow up?**
NICK: When I grow up, I'd like to find out all about the moon and all that.

Q: **Are there other children in your village?**
NICK: I'm the only child in the village except for my baby brother. He was one last Friday, I mean the Friday before last Friday.

Q: **Do you like to fight?**
NICK: I have quite a lot of fun when I fight. You better watch out for me, 'cause as soon as you're not looking, I like to dash up and put my hands in front and hit them against your back.

Q: **What do you think about girls?**
NICK: I don't answer questions like that.

Q: **If you could change the world, what would you do?**
NICK: If I could change the world, I'd change it into a diamond.

NICK

When he was ten, Nick won a scholarship to a Yorkshire boarding school.

Q: **Are you happy at the boarding school?**
NICK: In this village there's me and then the next oldest is Andrew there. That's it. I'm not unhappy living on the farm and going to this school and boarding there. I think it would be better than living at the farm all the time. I wouldn't like to live at the school all the time, either.

Q: **Do you want to take up farming?**
NICK: No, I'm not interested in it. I said I was interested in physics and chemistry; well, I'm not going to do that here.

Q: **Did your father want to be a farmer?**
NICK: I don't think he really wanted to be, but he got stuck with it, because my grandfather, he certainly probably wanted him to be a farmer, but I don't think my father wants me to be a farmer. My youngest brother [Christopher], the deaf one, if he can't do anything else, he could probably run a farm as a last resort.

Q: **Have you done much traveling?**
NICK: I've been to Leeds a couple of times. I haven't been to Manchester; I went to London when you did the first program, but that's the only time I've been.

Q: **Do you like money?**
NICK: Well, I mean almost everybody likes money. I don't like looking at money; it doesn't give any pleasure like that, but I certainly don't want to be poor or live in a slum. A person with one million pounds is not going to be more unhappy than a person with two million pounds.

Q: **What do you think about colored people?**
NICK: I don't care what color somebody is, unless they're blue, and I think that would be pretty peculiar, but you might find somebody yet. I don't care about color.

Q: **Do you believe in God?**
NICK: I'm not sure whether I really believe in God or not. I think to myself, Is there a God?, and I don't know—so I don't know.

Q: **Do you have a girlfriend?**
NICK: I thought that would come up, because when I was on the other one, somebody said, "What do you think about girls?" and I said, "I don't answer questions like that." Is that

the reason you are asking me? Well, what do you want me to say? I don't know what to say.

21

At twenty-one, Nick was in his second year at Oxford, where he was studying physics.

Q: **Do you have a girlfriend?**
NICK: The best answer would be to say that I don't answer questions like that; it was what I said when I was seven and it's still the most sensible—but what about them?

Q: **Well, you seemed at fourteen to be very shy of your whole sexual life. Has that changed?**
NICK: I've tried to make a change, yes. A very definite conscious effort not to be shy and to be more outgoing, and this is actually something I can point to in my own past and think, Yes, I did make my mind up here, here, and here that I was going to try and change this, this, and this. "This" being basically my confidence and my sort of approach to—well, to people in general.

Q: **Tell me about your studies.**
NICK: Well, I'm trying to be a physicist. Fill in the detail of whenever you meet somebody at university, the standing question is, "Where are you and what are you doing?" And my answer is, "I'm at Merton College and I'm doing physics."

Q: **So what career are you going to pursue?**
NICK: It depends whether I'll be good enough to do what I really want to do. I would like, if I can, to do research.

Q: **Are there any disadvantages in coming from a small place like this preparing yourself for Oxford?**
NICK: Well, it's a rather different background to go anywhere—Oxford, perhaps especially. It's a rather more firm foundation, I would have thought, as to your character, than being brought up in a city. It's a fixed reference point in a sense—that sort of earthy life-and-death cycle that you get living on a farm. If something dies, it rots and feeds back into the earth. Sometimes it's helpful. In a city, things that some people are very concerned about seem quite irrelevant.

Q: **Is there any strength of your father as a farmer that you think has been transmitted to you?**
NICK: Well, the sense of calmness in situations, you know. You take things as they come; you have to revise things. If the dogs are chasing the animals in the wrong direction, you just

have to put up with it; they won't do as they are told. You just become resigned to these things.

Q: **I suppose of all the seven-year-olds, the original ones, you are the big success.**
NICK: I'm not inclined to agree with that.

Q: **Why?**
NICK: Well, with what I've achieved I'm not really prepared to accept that I've done anything very special yet. I'd like to feel that, I'm hoping that I might at some stage, but I don't really think that I've done anything you can call a great success. It would seem really ridiculous to any of my friends who watch this if I said, "Christ, aren't I great? Look at me." I can't think of it in those terms. I mean, I haven't done anything that can be called a success, nothing out of the ordinary really.

Q: **What do you see as your strengths and weaknesses?**
NICK: I suppose that I behave rather after the fashion of the people I'm with. In some circumstances, I think that can be a weakness. I sometimes just wish I didn't because on occasions I think, Christ, you bloody fool, what are you doing now? And that sometimes disturbs me.

28 *At twenty-eight, as an assistant professor at the University of Wisconsin, Nick was performing experiments in an attempt to produce atomic energy free from radioactivity. He had married Jackie, whom he met when both were students at Oxford.*

NICK: The gas in these experiments is at a temperature comparable with that of the sun,
whereas in a power reactor it will be maybe ten times the temperature of the sun. We're trying to induce that gas to fuse until the fuse reaction gives off energy and produces the power that would be turned into electrical energy and sent out to the consumer.

Q: **How hot is it in there?**
NICK: In there, it's at about ten million degrees.

Q: **When did you come to America?**
NICK: I finished my degree in physics and then I went on to do a Ph.D., and having got the Ph.D.—it took some two-and-a-half years to get that, which was relatively quick—I went to work at the United Kingdom Atomic Energy Authority's Culham Laboratory, which is where they do fusion research, and that is what I've been aiming to do throughout my Ph.D. But when I got there, I got a big shock when I found that my standard of living went down when I started work, so when some people here offered me a job, I thought this might be a

good opportunity to go somewhere else where their research environment was a bit more vigorous. So I came here in November of 1982 into a blizzard. The university is substantially different from an English university for several reasons. It's a much bigger university: Oxford has 10,000 people; this has 40,000 people.

I guess the mixture of people who come here is different. A far bigger fraction of the population go to university here. Oxford is full of people who really are trying to prove something, I suppose, or be something—a lot of people with social or intellectual pretentions. You're less aware of that sort of thing here. On the other hand, the American system is much more like the comprehensive system in England would try to be. It takes many more people and gets a huge section of the population to a level where they are really technically very competent and can go out and make Silicon Valley work.

Q: **Jackie, why did you marry Nick?**
JACKIE: Nick was only seventeen when we first met and I knew he was a nice person. I found him very attractive, and he uses his intelligence in his relationship with me, which is very important. A lot of people can be very bright in their work but they don't apply it to the way they live their lives, and Nick does.

Q: **What about you, Nick? Why did you marry Jackie?**
NICK: Because I find her attractive; she's bright and independent.

JACKIE: If you'd been somebody who had had fixed ideas of a woman's role in marriage that meant dinner on the table at six every evening…

NICK: Didn't I tell you about that?

JACKIE: I think we would have had problems, or if one of us had not wanted children…

Q: **Where did you get all this brain power?**
NICK: All this brain power? I don't know. Did it just happen, all this brain power? That's a hard one to answer, because first I have to accept that I've got "all this brain power," and that's not the sort of thing I tend to go around saying, but I've always been interested, from a very early age, in technical or scientific things. When I was very young, I had a big picture book about the planets, and I thought this was wonderful. And I've just been interested in that sort of thing, in reading technical or scientific material, for a long, long time.

I was the only child of my age in my village, but I managed to spend my time talking to adults who were around. I remember looking at various natural phenomena and being intrigued to try to understand what made them tick.

I think that if I'd been in a city, I probably would have had more interaction with people and might have developed more skills in dealing with other kids—trying to become a reasonably well-adjusted person was, for me, a bit of a struggle for a while, and I was given a fantastic opportunity when I went to university, and that really saved my bacon.

Q: **What attracts you about America?**
NICK: It's an exciting place to be. There's a lot going on in terms of research and other things. I really came here to do research, but I think there are more opportunities and just a general feeling of more going on than I had previously.

The place is less hide-bound; it's less bureau-cratically tied down—so it's much easier to go out and get things done than in England.

Q: **Do you get lonely here?**
JACKIE: You just tend to get stuck into your everyday routine and you don't think about it. When you call home, then you realize how far away you are. And now it seems acute because both our families are getting older.

Even if you think in terms of seeing them once every two years, you're thinking about only ten times and that's awful. When you think in those terms, you realize, you know, you really are in exile.

Q: **Does it put a pressure on your relationship?**
JACKIE: No, I think it binds us together because we just have one another over here.

Q: **In 21UP, some of the people were saying that it was immoral to emigrate, immoral to leave. Do you have any feelings about that since you're the one who's left?**
NICK: In my position, I don't feel that I'm letting England down, because I don't think that England particularly wanted me there doing what I was doing. It had trained me marvelously; I'd gone through a wonderful educational system, particularly Oxford was a fantastic experience socially, and it was a great place to try and develop emotionally; and the academic standards there are absolutely superb.

Having trained in a very academic fashion there, I then went out to try and do something with all that training and found that society wasn't terribly interested in what I was trying

to do. So how can I feel that I'm betraying a country when it doesn't want me to do what it's trained me to do?

Q: **Are you thinking of having children?**
NICK: The big issue for us at the moment is how are we going to manage to have kids and run two careers? We don't want to miss out on the chance of having a significant career, and we don't want to miss out on the chance of having kids and to be involved in them.

Q: **But in those early formative years, would you be happy for your children to be brought up by Jackie, and Jackie not being able to give them full attention?**
NICK: Well, that's putting it in a rather strange way. This is an area where I pay lip service to the idea of equal shares on this, and it remains to be seen whether I would actually live up to my intentions.

JACKIE: There are several things, I think, to be said here. If we both work in academia, that will make life much easier because as things are at the moment in the States, if you have a computer at home, you can come in to teach and to give office hours to your students, but you can work half of the day from home.

But I don't want to be the person left behind while Nick flies in and shares an adult life with his children. I want to be there, too.

Q: **Is she difficult?**
NICK: At times, yes. Whenever we have an argument, she does have a tendency to ex-plode, I suppose—no, to get really miserable.

JACKIE: We've only been married four years; anything could happen. We could easily drift apart. There are so many pressures on people; you just have to work at it and that's why it's important that you have the same ideas — that you want the same kind of life.

Q: **What do you fight about?**

NICK: When we were in England, our big source of arguments was money. We were always squabbling about money, but that one mercifully seems to have gone away pretty well. We still disagree, but it isn't a major source of rows.

I've never really been aiming for money, and that, curiously enough, is why it was such a surprise when I found that my standard of living mattered to me when I finished university and I found that I couldn't afford what I'd been able to afford as a student. It suddenly caught up with me for the first time in my life that I really did care about how much money I was getting — and it had never occurred to me that I would.

JACKIE: When I first met you, I remember I thought that you were very idealistic and it was rather interesting when I asked you why you were working on fusion. You said you wanted to save the world.

NICK: That's right. I picked it because I thought it really was something that could be useful to people. Hopefully eventually.

Yes, it would be a disappointment if I didn't achieve very much, but I'm not worrying about it very much. I've just got to go out and make it happen.

35 *At thirty-five, Nick had become an associate professor at the University of Wisconsin.*

Q: **Now that you're more firmly established in the States, what differences do you see between Americans and the English?**

NICK: I think in general you'll find that Americans are much more determined to follow through on their ideas and much more upbeat about their chances of having success. You'll find that Americans looking at this film find the English people in it very low-key and lacklustre. Part of that is just they don't understand how the English communicate. If the English are saying something quite positive, they'll make some very moderate statement: "I'm quite pleased about this," or something, and that means, "I'm absolutely delighted" or "I'm over the moon" in American terms.

Q: **Is Madison a friendly place?**

NICK: Yes, very friendly. It's a fairly small little community and you get deer and things running through here, so it's kinda nice. If you walk into a shop here, or a store, as they

would call it, people are much more polite to you than they are in England. And it's not just a matter of being obsequious; they just try and be reasonably friendly and smile at you.

Q: **People saw the last film and thought, This marriage isn't going to work; it isn't going to last. Did you get that response?**

NICK: Well, it's actually such a mystery to me what they thought they were talking about that I really just don't relate to it at all. I just don't know why they said that. I mean, the sorts of things you were seeing was us trying to be very honest about it. That may have been the place in *28* where we probably were working hardest about really describing what things were like. I was just saying I sometimes just am very dull and neutral. Well, in that I think we were just trying to be really upfront and say, "This is what it's like, and we're work-ing very hard at it and hopefully it'll work out." If that sounds to somebody like it's in jeop-ardy, well that's their problem.

Q: **I understand your son Adam is now a year old. Tell me about him.**

NICK: The thing that I notice that's different, now that I have him—apart from just spending all the time I spend and the things we do—is I look at the world even when he's not there, and I find myself relating a lot to small children who remind me of him, to small children as a whole, and seeing them as being similar to him. And so they are tremen-dously important to me. I feel very protective and affectionate towards them.

Q: **Do you miss England?**

NICK: An awful lot, yeah. My parents managed to get over here a couple of times in the last two years, and Andrew, my middle brother, was here about two years ago, so that's pretty good going.

Christopher is the brother who is deaf, as you know, and his language skills are getting better. He can't hear essentially at all, so you can't really have a conversation on the phone. He'll get on the phone and tell you a bunch of stuff and you can understand most of it, so that's really nice.

Q: **Is it painful for you?**

NICK: Well, the thing that was emotional to think back on was the situation when he was probably a year old, and it was really becoming clear to everybody that, despite the fact that his doctor had originally insisted he wasn't deaf, that it became pretty clear that he was, and you know at the time, I just desperately was hoping it wouldn't be true, that somehow some sort of miracle would happen and he would turn out not to be. But then I told myself, Well, if he weren't, then he wouldn't be the same person and it would be wishing that the person didn't exist, so that wasn't the appropriate way to think about it.

Q: **Do you think you can build a life here?**

NICK: Well, you know, one is trying to, but it is very difficult being in a place where you're a long way away from all your background and you don't have any sort of support network. I mean, you have to fend for yourself, you keep thinking you're really being called on to show pioneer spirit.

I don't have this urge that you sometimes hear people saying that I want my child to have all the things that I didn't. I don't look back and think I was deprived. There were things that I had in a certain sense as a child which were not material things that I had but situations I was in and experiences that most children wouldn't have. Growing up on a farm and actually working on a farm and being in a situation of being told, "Clean out that calf shed," really has made me very determined to get things done and not give up halfway through something. It develops a streak of stubbornness that can be useful now. The trouble with me is that I tend to take the streak of stubbornness too far. I have to try and mellow out a bit.

42 *This interview took place in the Yorkshire Dales, where Nick grew up.*

Q: **It's incredible that it all started here, isn't it?**
NICK: Yes and no—you shouldn't underestimate what resources people have. Yorkshire farmers are very profound people. They are very smart people; they are businessmen in a really rough business, a really hard business that is in the process of dying out, and they are hanging in there by tooth and nail to try and keep things going. These are magnificent people. You shouldn't look at this little place and say, "How surprising that anything could emerge from here." I mean, these are fantastic people and you know you don't get better teachers anywhere else than we had. So no, it is not surprising.

Q: **What do you think you have learned about life here, in this environment?**
NICK: Just look at this place. It is utterly beautiful, but not beautiful in the pretty, cutesy way. It's very uncompromising and sometimes it is very tragic, but it makes other places you go seem rather trivial as well. And so I get a lot of confidence, I'm enormously proud of having come from here. You couldn't be more proud of where I come from, and the idea of being a Dales person is really terribly important to me.

Q: **What is it to be a Dales person?**
NICK: Well, it's not an easy place to live, and people have to struggle quite a lot to just live their lives and do their work. And so Dales people, I think, are very, very philosophical and they're quite profound, not trivial people. They just have a depth. A solidity.

Q: **Your folks are getting old now, your mum and your dad. Will you be coming back here many more times, do you think?**
NICK: I hope so. I'm going to try. Adam, my son, went straight up the hill, almost as if this was something he had been bred to do. And he

wouldn't stop. I mean, he just wanted to get up to the top, to the highest possible point, and look out and get photographs. He said, "I want to remember this, I may not come back here." I didn't know he was going to act like that. And he didn't get that from me. I didn't say that to him; that was his own idea. I thought he'd sort of gone to the heart of the matter there.

Q: **Do you wish he had had this kind of upbringing?**
NICK: There are lots of parts of it I wish he could have. I mean, there is a feeling of being toughened up and being prepared for things by it that I don't know how to give him, and I think about that and I don't know how to supply him with that. A child needs to feel that he or she can take on things and deal with them and have things that they can build on. And just having lived here gave me a feeling that I can take on other things.

Q: **Are you happy about bringing Adam up in America?**
NICK: In some ways yes, in some ways no. I mean, it is a mixed thing. He has advantages there and some disadvantages, and you try and make the best of it. He has access to things that we didn't here. He can have lessons in this, that, and the other, but he doesn't have a hill to run up, a sheep to chase and so on—and he clearly likes that.

Q: **How long since you've been back?**
NICK: I'm afraid I think it's been five years since I've been back here.

Q: **What's happening to the farming here?**
NICK: Well, I don't entirely know, but you only have to look around and see that every second house is a hotel, and I think it's great that it's accessible to people to come here to be tourists. The thing is, the farmers are responsible for keeping it in a form that anybody would want to look at it. And if the farming is dying out, it is not going to be very nice to visit.

If you pay someone to shear a sheep, you can't sell the wool for enough to pay the guy who sheared it, and you don't get much for our little scruffy sheep if you are selling them for meat. And cattle, of course, nobody is eating beef much right now. Even with the subsidies it's barely livable.

Q: **So your dad is packing it in.**
NICK: It hasn't been viable for a very long time. His father was just so deeply committed to farming, just believed in it, that there was no way he could do anything else. I think he rather pushed my father into doing it, but you know it was something that generations ago was a proud occupation. Now these are small farms; a lot of them are tenant farms. We're not talking about having hundreds of acres of rich, arable land.

So, yes, he's giving up the farm. He's retiring and the stock have been sold except for a very few that we have been feeding over the last day or two, and in February it will be completely turned over, I understand, to its owner, and that will be that. They moved a couple of days ago out of the farmhouse into a little cottage that they own. They've been refurbishing it and they've done a nice job. This was the cottage where they lived when I was born and it was not in terribly good shape before they started redoing it. It's very hard to keep these cottages at all warm, for instance.

Their health has not been the greatest. My father in particular has had a number of operations, and the National Health, when they got round to him, they seemed to have done a nice job. It just took a while and he was in tremendous pain with his hip and his knee. Well, they've done the hip and he's feeling a lot better, so that's just wonderful, but his health is a great concern.

Q: **Your brother won't take over on the farm?**
NICK: No, absolutely not, no.

Q: **What has happened with Christopher since we were last here?**
NICK: Well, Christopher is married, which is great. He has a very nice wife who is getting better and better at communicating with the deaf. He works in Skipton and he's taking some courses in computers.

Q: **What about Andrew?**
NICK: Andrew is a newspaper reporter. He is I think about to take a job near York. So that's great. I hope he just finds somewhere nice to live there because for it to be a pleasant job for him, he is going to need a base over there. He can't commute from here.

Q: **Would you ever think of coming back here yourself and living here?**
NICK: I do think about it. Again, I don't know quite how I'd manage. I couldn't come back here and work. As soon as I wasn't going to be a farmer, I couldn't live here anymore, and in a way choosing to leave here is like having your right arm ripped off. Maybe you could retire here, but people retiring somewhere where they haven't lived for forty years can be

a big mistake. So I don't know. It would be very hard to, and I do feel really wrenched away from a big part of my life here, and I don't know how to get back to it.

Q: **Does it make you emotional thinking about this?**
NICK: Very much so. I don't want to get too worked up about it, but yes, I feel very bereaved and somehow swindled that I can't be around here. And you know, it didn't seem like it was my choice. Didn't seem like I had any choice at all.

Q: **What about those who are left here, your brothers, your mum and your dad. Do you miss them?**
NICK: Yes, very much. My brothers can't work here, either; they are all off somewhere else. It's terrible not being able to be in touch with them as much. I don't want to say this, but I feel very guilty about not being here.

One of the reasons why I really felt driven to go through education was that I had this idea that somehow if I did, I'd be in a better place to try and help my family because goodness knows they need it. That really lit a fire under me to persevere.

Q: **Have you been able to look after them?**
NICK: I don't think I have done any more to look after them than just not actually take up any of their resources. If you ask my parents, they'd probably say they'd rather have me around and being a drain on the resources.

Q: **The feelings you get from here, would you call them spiritual values or what?**
NICK: There is a feeling of being in touch with nature. I mean, one of my jobs in spring, unfortunately enough, was burying dead

lambs. Now this is not pleasant obviously; it's really horrible. But that feeling of being part of the cycle—you look at trying to help them in being born; you look after them; you feed them; you deal with the ones that don't make it—and having dealt with that helps you to deal with other things. It's actually in some sense very unspiritual. It's all very down to earth and practical sometimes. But also when you go to the top of that hill and look out at the views you can get from there, it's desperately beautiful and moving.

Q: **Tell me about what has been happening at work over the last seven years since I last saw you in Madison.**
NICK: It's changed in a few ways. In addition to now being a full professor, I've been doing some administrative jobs. I've been associate chair of my department. I've been running admissions and dealing with student problems for the graduate program. We had a center from NSF [National Science Foundation] for basically using plasmas in industrial applications. Plasmas are ionized gases. That was funded to the tune of between two and three million dollars a year and it got shut down probably a year earlier than I would have expected because of conflicts in the center. As far as I know, it had nothing to do with me, but nevertheless that stream of money has gone away, so that we are going to have to look lively and replace that.

And I've spent the last year-and-a-half writing a couple of books. One about this business of using plasmas to process semi-conductors; that one's not quite finished.

And there is another one that was about semi-conductors.

Q: **Have your ambitions changed?**
NICK: They have a bit, because I think that I tend to be getting a bit less of a pure scientist and more looking for real impact. I mean, I always wanted to have an impact, to do something useful that was actually going to benefit people. I had this vision of people in ivory towers being cut off, doing stuff all their lives and having no effect on anybody whatsoever, and that was absolutely not what I wanted to do, and so I chose to go into this fusion business because I thought this would have a huge impact. When I was a teenager I read books that were all concerned about environmental catastrophes and I really wanted to do something that would make recycling and so on more practical—and one of the things you really need to recycle is lots of electricity.

Q: **Do you still have your passion?**
NICK: I'm very driven to work on what I am doing. There are things that I am doing that I think should be useful short term, and there are mathematical methods that I am working on that I think are fairly profound. And so I am still a workaholic. Most of it has to be done after midnight when it is quiet.

Q: **Are you optimistic that you can make a difference?**
NICK: Well, I think that the sort of difference I'm thinking in terms of making is not a very grandiose one at the moment. I mean, most times when scientists do something spectacular, they stumble on something that is lucky and it is very hard to plan for these sort of

things; otherwise more of us would do it. I try and identify important problems to work on, but even that's hard. It's hard even to know the important problem to work on. And most people don't even make a strenuous effort to do that. But I'm not expecting to be reported in newspaper headlines anytime soon. That is not the limit of my ambition, but it's just trying to be realistic. I'm just about to try and settle for reasonable, small victories.

Q: **Tell me about marriage and children in the last seven years.**
NICK: Well, the last seven, eight years have been dominated by children, or one child, and I think that my life is focused much more on my wife and child. Emotionally, it centers round them more than work. I still work an enormous amount but they are much more the focus of what I am thinking about or fretting about than work is. So that's probably quite a big change for me.

Q: **Why only one child?**
NICK: Well, there's a couple of reasons. One is that these silly jobs we have demand such an amount of time and such a commitment that it is hard to fit in one. Also, he's such a lively person and he demands such a lot of attention that he makes it hard to find time for another.

Q: **So you don't want another?**
NICK: I would dearly love to have another one. I actually adore children. I think two is as many as I could legitimately hope for and as many as I could ever manage, but if I had to say my ideal number, it would probably be two.

Q: **Are you getting on well, you and Jackie?**
NICK: I would say very well, yes. In many ways we are very compatible. We are both a bit too forceful, but the thing is—I hate to say this—we both come from backgrounds where not everybody expected us to get a tremendous education, and in order to get an education in our backgrounds you do have to be quite single-minded. We couldn't have got this far if we hadn't have been like that.

We spend a lot of time trading off who is looking after our son because the other one has to rush off to work. We're doing a little bit better on that but it's very wearing; we are always tired, we are always short of sleep, always cranky, always stressed out.

Q: **What does Jackie do?**
NICK: Jackie is a professor of journalism. She's just got tenure, and she does research in advertising and in related areas and in what she would call "media convergence." She's interested in psychological aspects of advertising and how they should be regulated and controlled. She did some stuff which I thought was really fascinating on political advertising and how it works for women candidates, or how it can work against them, and what their strategies should be.

She's a wonderful teacher and she gets tremendous ratings and you can hardly walk down the street in Madison without being stopped by all the students. She had a class of 400 students last semester. It's another reason why we are tired. I mean, it takes hours to even write down their grades.

Q: **Is money an issue with you, a problem for you?**

NICK: Money is not an overriding issue. I haven't managed to save any, but it's not my number-one thing that I worry about at the moment. I have a grumble about how much is getting spent every month when I get the credit card bill, but I'm just trying not to be such a grouch about it and not be quite so anxious about it. No, so that's probably not my number-one concern.

Q: **Where is home to you now, then?**
NICK: What a nasty question, Michael! The easy answer is probably it's not a physical location at all. I mean, that's the problem: I don't really feel like I belong anywhere at the moment except with the people who are closest to me.

Q: **It's hard being away from your roots, isn't it?**
NICK: Terribly hard. It's hard in lots and lots of ways. I mean, if you go to an alien culture, you don't know what's going on around you half the time. It's really strange to go to a different country: people don't send out the same signals. When we do something, it doesn't mean the same thing. So even when you think you speak the same language, you scarcely do. Everything from good manners to just more subtle clues if you meet somebody. Somebody who has grown up in the culture can tell a lot about somebody—who they are and what they are likely to be like—very quickly from little clues, and it's like being suddenly tone deaf and color-blind, both of which I am.

Q: **Do you imagine you will spend the rest of your life in America?**
NICK: I don't know the answer to that, and whenever anybody asks me I just give them some noncommittal answer. It's very hard to imagine being able to come back here and I think about it a lot, but I haven't seen the way to do it yet.

SUE

The daughter of a cabinet maker and a part-time machinist, Sue grew up in the East End. The family's house was on a quiet street, opposite a bridge; Sue's parents and grandmother slept upstairs, while Sue's bedroom was downstairs, facing the yard. "I was really frightened of that yard," she recalls. "Maybe it was because the toilet was out there—we didn't have an indoor bathroom." As a child, Sue developed a fear of vampires, and to this day, she says, "I still have to have something round my neck when I'm asleep."

An only child, Sue attended the Susan Lawrence School with Jackie and Lynn, other participants in the UP series. "At the time," she says, "I don't remember being that bothered about not having any brothers or sisters. I do remember being jealous of Jackie with all her sisters. But the only way it really affected me was that it made me decide I'd never do it to my own child."

7

Q: **What do you think about fighting?**
SUE: Well, sometimes we go out and play nicely with the boys, and sometimes we go out and argue with the boys.

14

Like Jackie and Lynn, Sue had the choice of going to a comprehensive or a grammar school.

Q: **Why did you choose a comprehensive school?**
SUE: I just didn't feel like going to grammar school. Comprehensive school just seemed more friendly.

Q: **What advantages has a comprehensive school got?**
SUE: Oh, especially this school, it's got everything, everything you could want.

Q: **How do you spend your free time?**
SUE: I like serials—I like *Peyton Place* and *Crossroads*.

Q: **Have you ever been abroad?**
SUE: I have. Spain, Gibraltar, and Casablanca. That was interesting.

Q: **Have you got any boyfriends?**
SUE: That's personal, ain't it?

Q: **What do you think of rich people?**
SUE: They can be all right, but I don't like people who are too posh. They look down on everybody else; they think they are better.

I don't see why they should have all the luck when people worked all their lives and haven't got half the money that they have. It just doesn't seem fair. Some people don't know what to do with their money, so they spend it, waste it.

Q: **Is money important to you and your friends?**
SUE: It does mean a lot to us now, with the clothes and the new fashions and everything, doesn't it? Midis and that—you need money.

Q: **Do you want to be rich?**
SUE: I don't mind. I'd like to stay as I am. I don't want to be too rich; I don't want to be too poor.

Q: **Do you believe in God?**
SUE: Well, if you are brought up to believe in Him, you do.

Q: **What are your goals for the future?**
SUE: Just to be content with what I'm doing and be happy with it, and to know where I'm going, and to remember fondly what I've done.

Q: **There is a danger that you will get married in your early twenties and have children quickly and be stuck at home. Have you had any thoughts on that?**

SUE: I don't think I'd get married too early. I'd like to have a full life first, and meet people... before you commit yourself to a family.

21 *At twenty-one, Sue was single and working in London.*

Q: **Tell me about your work.**
SUE: I work for a travel company. I don't deal with the public; I deal with groups and company groups. Incentive holidays abroad and conferences, that sort of thing, which I like, because I like foreign places. I do quite a bit of typing, but a lot of my work is involved in making bookings and dealing with hotels abroad.

Q: **In admitting that you're not a career girl, does it mean that you are therefore looking for a family?**
SUE: Well, I don't know. I suppose I am, but everything's not that cut and dried. It's not either a career or a family: it's what's in the middle. I mean, am I just going to carry on as I am now—and end up on the shelf? Or am I just going to get married? Could be any day.

Q: How did you feel about attending Jackie's wedding?

SUE: I was pleased I was there. It seemed the right place to me. I've known her a long while.

Q: What are your thoughts on marriage?

SUE: Marriage didn't appeal to me. I've still got my ideals about marriage; I don't know what it's all about, obviously, so I've still got pictures of cozy evenings indoors.

I've got a lot to learn about marriage.

28 *Sue was twenty-four when she married Billy, a gas fitter. At twenty-eight, Sue was living in a council house in the East End with Billy and their son William.*

Q: Tell me about your decision to get married.

SUE: When I got married, the primary reason was because I wanted to have a child. The two to me went together. I can understand Jackie's decision [not to have children], because I think there's still a lot of pressure put on young married couples to have children, as though it's expected of them. And I think it's all wrong—it's just a personal decision that everyone's entitled to make. And knowing what it does to your life, I can completely understand someone who decides not to.

Q: How does married life contrast with single life?

SUE: I'm lucky, I expect, because I still manage to do my own thing. I've got a husband who lets me do what I want and a mum who helps me out, you know. I do a part-time job, which is enough for me, because I don't think I could cope with a full-time job and wouldn't want to, personally.

I had a good time up till I was twenty-four, and I think that to get married young, there must be things that you miss. You must miss that crucial stage of being yourself—because the minute you get married, you're no longer a single being, you're a partnership and that should be the idea behind it.

Q: Do you get depressed by money problems?

SUE: It was hard first of all when I gave up work—from having a fairly high salary to nothing was hard. But you get used to it. Whatever your circumstances are, you live in them, you get used to them and you cope. Everybody does.

Q: So you don't feel bitter about a society that maybe gives one stratum more opportunities than another?

SUE: No, not bitter.

I think that we all could have gone any way that we wanted to at the time within our capabilities. I mean, we chose our own jobs—we were able to choose our own jobs quite freely.

Q: **Looking back, do you think you made the right choice when you decided to go to a comprehensive school?**

SUE: My mum knew I could go to grammar, and I decided that I didn't want to, and she encouraged me in the choice that I made. And right or wrong, that was my choice—as much as I was capable of making a decision. And I enjoyed myself.

Q: **Do you have any regrets about it?**

SUE: No, no. You can only have regrets about things if you're not happy with the way you are.

35 *At thirty-five, Sue was working part time at a building society. She and Billy divorced when she was thirty-two.*

Q: **Tell me about your life since you were twenty-eight.**

SUE: Just after we had made the last film, I had Kathryn, and when she was about a year,

the marriage started to sort of dissolve round us, really, and we decided to go our separate ways. I've never sat down and thought what it was: was it this, was it that? I just knew it wasn't working, and the discussion really was the best way of splitting up rather than why we were splitting up. It was really strange— I think it seemed so obvious to both of us that it was probably easier to do than it should have been.

I think that women want more out of life now; that is basically why they won't put up with a less-than-happy marriage. The number of people in my situation—not single parents as such, but divorced single parents—is unbelievable. And for people of my mum's generation, it's still rare, very rare.

Q: **Why did you have a child out of a marriage that wasn't working?**

SUE: Because I wanted to have more than one child—it was a thing about being an only child myself. I was always jealous of other children that had brothers and sisters when I was

growing up, and I didn't want to have more than one child with two different fathers. I think that a brother and sister should have the same mother and the same father; that is my ideal.

Q: **Has the divorce been hard on the kids?**

SUE: I would hate to think it was tough on the kids. William used to say, "Why isn't Daddy living here anymore?" and I would say to him, "Well, you know how you and Kathryn argue and get on each other's nerves? Well, that's how Daddy and I are. We just find that we're happier if we're not living in the same house."

Q: **How did you feel about living off Social Security after you and Billy split up?**

SUE: I hated it. Really hated it. Perhaps it's old-fashioned values. I mean, Mum and Dad have certainly never been in that situation, but then my mum and dad have never been single parents, either. So you have to do what's best for you and the children.

Everything's changed for me 'cause I'm now supporting myself a lot more than I was a year ago.

Q: **Do you socialize much?**

SUE: I have a regular one night a week when I can go out. It just happens to be that in this particular circle, most of my friends are separated or are divorced. You have common problems, so sometimes it's easier because you recognize each other's problems with baby-sitters. You know it's not always possible to drop everything and go out.

Q: **Are you ready for a long-term relationship?**

SUE: I don't think you're ever ready for a long-term relationship. Either it happens to you or it doesn't. I certainly wouldn't kick one in the teeth if it crept up on me—yeah, why not?

Q: **Do you have any regrets?**

SUE: We've all got little secret dreams. I mean, I loved drama at school—I loved to sing, along with millions of others, so I would have liked to have carried that further. It was discussed at one stage, you know, going to drama school and pursuing it, but I really at the time didn't want to give up work and income as a young person. As a young person, I was quite enjoying myself. Didn't want to risk all that to follow the dream.

Q: **So are these good times, Sue?**

SUE: Not particularly, no. I've got two lovely children now, but it's just another crossroads for me. I don't know which way I'm going to go, what's going to happen. I'm on my own, basically. I'm starting again.

42 Q: **Tell me what's happened since I last saw you at thirty-five.**

SUE: Oh, goodness. Nothing dramatic happened in the last seven years. I'm still single and the children have grown enormously. I am still living in the same place, so there's been no moves, although I have bought the house now rather than just renting it. So I suppose that's something to work on, something to build on. But I haven't actually done anything to the house yet—there's plans but nothing's actually been done yet.

Emotionally, obviously, I've had some relationships—some long ones, some short ones. Met some nice people, but nothing permanent.

Q: **Why's that?**

SUE: Because I think when you get to my age
—or perhaps it's just me—I don't know. I've
never been able to settle unless I've thought it
was right. I mean, there have been relationships where I could have settled, but they did-
n't feel quite right, so I've always come away
and pulled away and just waited until the right
one comes along. If they ever do.

Q: **Are you asking too much of a relationship,
do you think?**

SUE: Maybe. It's probably difficult. I mean,
I've got two children, and that's a lot for
anyone. It's never caused me any problems;
no one's ever said, "Oh, I can't get involved
with you because you've got two children."
I suppose it does happen, but it's never
happened to me. I've had some relationships
where the situation just wasn't right, and
although I've been happy for a while, I've
taken a sort of step back and thought, Well,
this has got to stop.

I'm with someone now, which is nice. It
feels nice, it feels right, but it's early yet.

Q: **Do you enjoy this kind of life, or does it get you
down, this relationship following relationship?**

SUE: Deep down, I probably wish I wasn't
having to do this. I mean, I'd like to be married
and have a steady relationship. But I'm the type
of person who likes to go out and have a good
time, so it's not that hard for me. But I think as
you get in your forties, you start thinking, Well,
maybe I should slow down a bit. You don't
know what's round the corner, do you?

Q: **Tell me how the children are doing.**

SUE: They keep me busy. They are really, really,
really good kids. I mean, they're at a funny age.
William is fifteen, doing his GSCE [General
Secondary Certificate of Education], so I'm
trying to make him study. He's always been
extremely bright, but he's discovered computers in a big way, and he tends to spend a lot
more time on that than he should, probably.
He's not quite as enthusiastic about school as
he used to be, but he's doing really well.

He's had a bad year, actually, William.
He had an operation earlier this year. He had
a lump in his neck; we had various opinions.
They thought it was a cyst, and it was quite
noticeable to him, particularly because he's so
tall and thin, and he wanted it gone. The

worst moment was when we went to see a specialist, just me and him. I'll never forget it. We sat down and he said, "Right. Bear in mind this could be a tumor." That was the first words out of his mouth. And my eyes, my mouth—I just filled up and I looked at William. He's very calm, he's very together, but I thought, What is going through his mind? Then the doctor said that it could also be a cyst. He had every test under the sun. And then he examined him and said, "Well, actually now I think it is a cyst of some sort." And I thought, Well, why didn't you examine him first instead of terrifying us?

It turned out just to be a normal cyst that happened to be near William's thyroid. It didn't affect him at all, but he's got a scar now which is obviously going to take time to heal.

Q: **Has it been hard bringing up a boy without a father?**

SUE: I don't think of it like that. He's very easygoing and he speaks his mind, as I do. That's the way I bring them up; we're very open with each other. And he sees his father occasionally, not as often as I would like, probably. I mean my ex, Bill, might ring up and say, "Can I take them out?" but they won't be there. When they are little, it's easier. They can have a regular time when they see their dad—which they did. But now that they are older, it's trying to fit in with their schedule rather than the other way around.

Q: **So you don't think he's missed having a dad?**

SUE: Probably, but I don't know how it's affected him. My dad's there; my children probably owe a lot to my mum and dad. I

mean, my mum and dad have been absolutely brilliant with them. The way that they behave is mostly down to my mum and dad, because they've done a good job and they've helped me out enormously—not just financially, but emotionally, bringing them up.

Q: **Has the money been tough?**

SUE: Money has been extremely tough. I've always worked, but anyone who's got teenagers knows how expensive it is, and there are times when I can't quite manage what I'd like to with them, especially school trips and things like that. I can't say they're greedy kids; they're just normal. They want things and they can't understand why they can't always have them. Particularly with the designer label thing that's going on. Especially with Kathryn, everything has got to have a name on it or she won't wear it, you know.

Q: **Is it scary thinking of the future in terms of money and you working?**

SUE: I don't worry about it. I've survived this far. I suppose with William being fifteen, he's going to carry on with his education and hopefully do his A levels, because he can and he should. What he's going to do, I don't know. He keeps changing his mind. It will be something to do with computers probably, and no, I don't worry about it—particularly because you can't. I've got certain little savings plans for them and policies that all come out when they're twenty-one, and hopefully things for when they get married or if they want a car. There are times that are hard when you are on your own, but hopefully I've got a few things put by that will help me out.

Q: **And what about Kathryn? Tell me about her.**
SUE: Kathryn is very much like me. My house is completely full of girls, constantly. I mean, it's like, "Who can stay tonight?" and "Where is she going tonight?" Very rarely is she in on her own. She's always got someone with her, four or five people sometimes, and she loves to be out with her mates. She's more into boys and dressing up and looking nice and that sort of thing.

She likes the karaoke—they both like it, actually. We went on holiday to Spain just for a week, the three of us, which was quite scary, because I'd never done that before. And we had a wonderful time. We went out and we found a nice bar with a karaoke and we were all singing together, and we had a wonderful time.

Q: **Why was it scary?**
SUE: Well, because I had visions of them both wandering off, finding friends, which they do quite easily, and leaving me. But we made friends, sat around the pool with people, and we had a really good time.

Q: **Were they brought up like you were brought up?**
SUE: Course they weren't, because there was only me. But the values are very much the same: I try to keep them on an even keel and to know what's acceptable and what isn't, and that's all that you can do. Their personalities are very different. Kathryn is doing well at school, but she's not into it like William. I mean, she just goes through it—she does what she has to do. She's bright but she does what she has to do rather than look to the future.

Q: **What do you want her to do that you didn't do?**

SUE: Everything, everything. I just want them both to travel and to do as much as they can, but she loves babies and she keeps saying, "Mum, I want a baby." And I say, "Don't even think about it," you know, but she's obsessed with babies. I think it's a thing that girls go through when they are that age—twelve.

Q: **What do you want them to do differently from what you did?**
SUE: With William, I want him to have a really satisfying career. Something that he really enjoys, which is something that I've never really had. I've had jobs that I like—I've never done something I really hated—but nothing that really stimulated me. I think that for him, I would love that—well, for both of them. I think he can go far if he puts his mind to it. You know, he may go to university—we have talked about it—if he does well. He's capable of it. With Kathryn, she talks about doing things like hairdressing and girlie things, 'cause she doesn't really know what she wants to do yet. She just wants to enjoy herself at the moment, and I can remember being the same when I was her age. We'll have to wait and see with Kathryn; I don't know which way she's going to go.

Q: **What sort of advice does a mum give her girl about men?**
SUE: What sort of advice? Never go out with a man whose eyebrows meet in the middle or wears brown shoes with black trousers. No—I mean, I don't know. I think the main thing I can do for her is to be there and listen to her and give her the benefit of my experience, but that probably won't help an awful lot. But I think that that is the best you can do as a

mum, because she'll make mistakes—we all make mistakes—but that's the best I can do. I can't warn her or tell her what I think, because she'll find her own way. My job is, I think, to be there and help her out when she needs it.

Q: **And how do you handle having different boyfriends with the two of them?**
SUE: Well, the funny thing is I have never really got them involved in boyfriends. I have had two fairly long relationships, and they met one of them and they got to know him. But they were younger then; that was quite a while ago. Since then, I made a mistake: they met one of the men I went out with for a while, and they got quite attached to him. And when I finished with him, they were more upset than I was. So I thought, Well, this isn't right, this isn't good.

I've never had anyone stay in the house when they've been there—I've never done that and I suppose I've been lucky, because I've always had my own time anyway, because my mum and dad have always sort of taken the kids off my hands maybe one night or a weekend or something. So I've had time to myself, but I've never really put it in their face, never. The fella I'm seeing now is probably the closest I've ever got to that, because as I say, it feels right. They are older now, anyway. They accept things. They could have made my life a nightmare if I'd really got them too involved in that, so I never have.

Q: **You've never thought of getting married again just for the kids?**
SUE: No, I would never do that. If I get married again, it will be for me first, and then obviously, hopefully, they will benefit from it as well.

Q: **You're one of the few single parents in the film. How is that?**
SUE: I've been a single parent for a long while, and I've brought them up on my own, really, 'cause Kathryn was only two when Bill left. It's been extremely hard, and sometimes it's been very lonely. The early days were the worst. Definitely. When they were ill or when they were worried or changing schools, making decisions. But I am quite strongwilled, so probably the decisions I made I would have made anyway, whether I'd been married or not. I put them in a school—which isn't the local school—because it was a better school, and I had to fight to get them both in there. Times like that, it would have been nice to have someone, you know, a partner to share those sorts of things with. But as the years go by, I think you get used to it.

Q: **Are there times when you've just said, "I can't"?**
SUE: There have been times when I've just wanted to lock myself in the bedroom and let someone else take over, but it doesn't happen. It never has happened, and so we just go from day to day. And if we're going through a bad patch, then we just get through it.

Q: **How do you deal with the bad patches?**
SUE: Well, you don't have any option, do you? I think the hardest thing is when they are ill, you know. When William was ill with his operation, that was quite scary; that would have been wonderful to have someone there with me. But at that time, I'd been on my own for so long that it would probably have annoyed me having to be with someone. At least this way, as I have got used to it, I can sort of get through it my own way.

Q: **You've never moved out of the East End. Why's that?**

SUE: Because I've never been able to. I mean, I've never really had this burning desire to move. There are much nicer places to live—I know that—but time tends to run away with you. I think maybe I am more likely to move in the next few years than I ever have been. Now they are sort of coming to the end of their major schooling years and I've bought the house now, and it's something I've got to build on. So probably—well, hopefully—I may do it in the next five or ten years, something like that. But until now, I have never been able to. I sort of live from month to month on my wages and there is never a lot left to save for major expenditure like that.

Actually, I've got two friends that live in the same street, and everyone's quite close to me, and we all meet in the same places, so for me it's still a nice place to be. You know, I've been single, so it's nice to have people round you. Starting afresh somewhere new on my own probably would have been a lot harder.

Q: **And has the neighborhood changed?**

SUE: Absolutely. It's unbelievably different. The shops that you grew up with have gone; they've been replaced. The people are different; the community is different. The schools I went to are now completely changed.

Q: **In what way?**

SUE: Well, it's difficult to say without sounding racist, but the thing is that now there are certain areas in the East End where I suppose you could say that we're the ethnic minority. The people, the generations that have grown up in the East End—we are the minority. And that's what's different, really. The shops have changed. They cater more for that side of the community than for us, you know.

Q: **And does that worry you?**

SUE: It's not worrying, but it's different. You've got to learn to adapt. I'm quite lucky in that I work with people from all round the world, and I mix with all sorts of cultures, and probably one helps me with the other.

Q: **Do you think it's true that England is a class society?**

SUE: Yes, it probably is true, but I don't think it matters as much anymore. I don't think people are as intimidated by an upper class anymore. You know, years ago it was very much, "You know your place," but I think you don't have to know your place anymore. You can do anything you want, within reason.

There are some areas you will never get into. I have met some really interesting people through my work that are of a higher class, and they talk to me and they describe things, and you know you will never be a part of that circle. But do you want to be, really? I don't want to be. I wouldn't be comfortable there; I would never be accepted.

Q: **What fears do you have for the children and their future?**

SUE: The biggest fear I probably have—it's a basic one, really—I just wish that they could find a cure for AIDS. I wish they could do that, because I never had that fear when I was growing up. I'm a worrier anyway, and I think Kathryn's a bit of a worrier, but wouldn't it be lovely if they didn't have that to worry about? They could just grow up and be normal and not have to worry about that. There are enough things to worry about without that.

Q: **Do you feel optimistic about the future?**

SUE: Yes. I'm always optimistic about the future. Always am—things can only get better.

PAUL

Paul spent his early years in London, where he lived with his father (a tailor), his mother, his Auntie May, and his older brother Grahame. When their parents separated, Paul and Grahame were sent to a children's home in Middlesex—the same home where Symon, another participant in the UP series, was living. "I honestly don't have that many memories going back then," says Paul. "I can remember bits and pieces, but they're only silly little things, like making our beds in the dormitories and having hot chocolate and buns for supper now and then. I would say I was unhappy at the children's home," he reflects, "but I wasn't in there for a long time. My father was saying the other day he doesn't even think it was twelve months."

7

Q: **Would you like to get married, Paul?**
PAUL: No.

Q: **Tell me why not.**
PAUL: Say you had a wife. Say you had to eat what they cooked you. And say I don't like greens—well, I don't—and say she said, "You'll have to eat what you get." So I don't like greens, and if she gives me greens, that's it!

Q: **What do you think about the children's home?**
PAUL: Well, I don't like the big boys hitting us and the prefects sending us out for nothing—and the monitors up in the washroom shouldn't send us out when there's no talking. I wasn't talking today, and Brown sent me out for nothing.

Q: **What do you think of fighting?**
PAUL: If they fight me—if somebody comes up and starts a fight—then I think it serves them right.

Q: **What do you think about money?**
PAUL: I've got twenty-three threepenny pieces, and I don't know how many halfpenny pieces I've got now.

Q: **Do you want to go to a university?**
PAUL: What does "university" mean?

Q: **What do you want to be when you grow up?**
PAUL: I was going to be a policeman, but I thought how hard it would be to join in.

When he was fourteen, Paul had moved with his brother, father, and stepmother to a suburb of Melbourne, Australia.

Q: Were you happy at the children's home in England?
PAUL: We didn't mind that, really, because we didn't know what was going on—because we were a bit young.

Q: What do you remember of England?
PAUL: It seemed to be raining all the time. I wouldn't stake my life on it, because I can't remember very much.

Q: Are you keen on sports?
PAUL: Basketball appeals to me most. With this school, I'm one of their best players in Form Two, but when I get into a team, they make me look as though I can't play.

Q: What career are you interested in?
PAUL: Well, I was going to become a bank accountant, but it's more booktaking than maths, and that was the main reason I was thinking about becoming a panel beater

[repairing damage to bodywork on vehicles]. And I don't know why, you know, I've stopped thinking about that; I just haven't made my mind up yet. I was going to be a phys.-ed. teacher, but one of the teachers told me that you had to get up into university.

Q: Would you like to get married?
PAUL: I'd prefer to be alone, really. I wouldn't mind living with my brother, but otherwise I'd prefer to live alone.

Paul left school when he was sixteen and entered a bricklaying course. At twenty-one, he was working as a junior partner for a firm of bricklayers in Melbourne and living with Susan, his girlfriend.

Q: Tell me about your job.
PAUL: The job I'm in—I'm in bricklaying—I enjoy it, it interests me, and I'm very content at work. In June last year I was made a junior partner. That was through circumstances, but I look at it this way: I'm not great at bricklaying, but if my boss didn't think I was good enough, he would never have made me a junior partner. As to the job, you know, you build a house and you turn around and look at it and say, "I did that."

Q: When you look at yourself, what do you think your strengths and weaknesses are?
PAUL: I find it hard to express emotions most of the time. Well, I'm getting on top of that more now. You know, just the simple things—to say to Susan, you know, "I love you." Something like that, I can tell you about it.

I really haven't been able to say it freely to Sue, you know. That's a weakness.

Q: **What fears do you have for the future?**
PAUL: To me, it is a dream to be totally happy. I mean, I don't think you can expect that.

Q: **How would you define happiness? What is it?**
PAUL: Well, basically to me, it's the will to live. I literally love life and I love people, and I think before, I didn't. I mean, when I was fourteen, I said—I've forgotten what the question was—but I said something about I want to be alone, and when I said that, I know even now I meant that. If someone were to drop me out in the Sahara Desert, I probably would have been happier, more or less, if you get the point. I'm not like that now. I like being around people; I don't like doing things by myself.

I've started to think, Well, now, I'm not a no-hoper, because really I think that's always what I've thought of myself. I know I didn't have much confidence in myself. I've always lacked confidence. I still do to a certain extent, but nothing like I did, say, when I was fourteen.

Q: **What would you like to be doing in, say, seven years?**
PAUL: All I want out of life is to be happy—and when I say happy, I want to be happily married as well, because I can't say I don't want to get married, because I think I do. But I want to be happily married, you know, and therefore I want to be sure.

28 *Paul and Susan married shortly after the filming of* 21 UP. *At twenty-eight, they were living in a working-class suburb of Melbourne with their two children, Katie and Robert.*

Q: **What was it that you fell in love with? What is it about him?**
SUSAN: His helplessness, I suppose. It was the mothering instinct in me just to pick him up and cuddle him. He's also very good-looking, I think, but he doesn't agree with me. In the summer, he's got this cute little bum in shorts!

Q: **Back in your early twenties, you bought an old van and spent seven months traveling through Australia. Tell me about that experience.**
SUSAN: I think it brought us closer together, because we really got to know each other and really relied on each other so much.

PAUL: I'd never been so relaxed in my life—I felt a lot more confident in myself. Just great fun, really. No pressures or worries, you know. Everything was forgotten.

SUSAN: We really went out in the middle of nowhere, where we had to carry our own petrol and our own water to do us for the three or four days that we were out that way. While we were up in Carnarvon, we went and stayed on a sheep station up there with our friend from Melbourne. And it was about a million acres, just under a million acres, the sheep station.

When we got to Perth, I was ready to fly home. Being together so much, it was hard, but then we settled down, and we must have settled down really well, 'cause I got pregnant. So something must have been going right.

It gave us our own peace of mind that we could now settle down and have a family, that we had done something; we hadn't just been nobodies and lived in suburbia all our lives. We'd done something that we were proud of, that we'd accomplished on our own.

Q: **Are you happy here in Australia?**
PAUL: I love the place, you know. I find it hard to put into words, really. You've got the country, you've got bush, outback, you can do more or less anything you want, I think, here— whether you do that in England, I don't know.

Q: **How would you compare life here to what you might have in England?**
PAUL: We've got a lot more than we would have had in England from what other people tell us. But there again, when it comes to work, I don't sit down on my backside. I'll go and chase it. So it's hard to say.

The family's going to come first, but I'm still going to be working and we'll progress, you know.

Q: **What's been happening with your work?**
PAUL: I went out on my own as a subcontractor not long after the last show, but then I started with a partner. I organized everything,

I bought all the equipment, 'cause I didn't want to be dependent on someone else. Things didn't work out between the two of us —he was a bit lazy.

Q: **Do you have the right temperament, do you think, to run your own business?**
PAUL: If you're talking about employing other people, I'm not hard enough. I'm a little bit slow working out things on the job—not particularly the laying of the bricks, but fairly slow thinking when you've got to work something out. I think that'll end up being my job for life, probably. Not that I want it that way, 'cause it gets harder as you get older, I think.

Q: **Do you feel there's any conflict ahead if Sue wants a job and a career?**
PAUL: Really, I think Susan will probably be the best one to be a businesswoman, and I'll stay home.

Q: **Are you ambitious for your children, Paul?**
PAUL: I said something about wanting Robert to be a brain surgeon but that was a joke. I

mean, if he's a brain surgeon, good and well—but it'd be nice to let them go one step up from us, I think.

Put it this way: I hope he's better at schoolwork than I was, so that he's got a choice, 'cause, really, the educational standard I got, I didn't have a choice.

At the moment I'm pretty happy with Katie. I've got fears for Robert because he's struggling a little bit. He's only been at school for two years; he's in grade one, and he's had three teachers already that say they don't know how to motivate him.

Q: **What regrets do you have about your education, then?**
PAUL: I didn't work hard enough. I was just very lazy at school, you know. If you're lazy and you don't work at school, you suffer for it. There needs to be a little more discipline.

If private schools are better, you'd be far better off spending your money and sending your kids there than getting a video or a new television, swimming pool, or something like that, I think.

Q: **What else do you want for your kids that you didn't have?**
PAUL: A happier family, I think. Don't get me wrong: I wasn't miserable, but I think it could have been better. I think that'd be one of the most important things.

Q: **Do you have any regrets about the fact that you weren't closer to your father when you were younger?**
PAUL: Yes, I suppose. I mean it's all wasted time in a way, I suppose. He was always there; I could always talk to him, but it was different.

We were sort of distant friends and all; we always got along fairly well. We didn't see much of each other.

He said actually to his wife Barbara that he missed out on his own children and he's not going to miss out on these.

Q: **What mark has it left on you, the fact that you were brought up within a bad marriage?**
PAUL: Divorcing your wife, what does it get you? It messes up your own life; it messes up the kids' lives, wife's life. I don't think half the people that get divorced even think about it properly.

Q: **You seemed such a sad little boy.**
PAUL: That's me, that. I was pretty long-faced. I was like that sometimes out here, too—always getting knocked up.

Q: **Does he eat greens now?**
SUSAN: He loves them, he loves them, he loves them!

 At thirty-five, Paul and a partner had started a business that specialized in underpinning foundations.

Q: **Tell me about your work.**
PAUL: Well, I'm more of a tradesperson than a business person, you know. I've never had any business training, and if I've got a natural ability, I probably haven't used it.

I think the confidence was never there—it might run in the family sort of thing.

SUSAN: I think maybe it's the lack of security he felt as a child, perhaps; that's my theory, my theory alone. I mean, that's the old thing, isn't it, when one of your parents are taken away from you, you lack security.

Katie now has this saying, "Oh, you know me, I'm hopeless," and it's just Paul, you know: "Oh, you know me, I can't do this." And it's sort of like this defeatist attitude.

He has got better. I think as you get older, mature, confidence does come, to a point.

PAUL: I really went through a stage—it's so stupid, 'cause I was only a bricklayer—like I failed. Something happened with that job, and maybe I did start to look at what we had and think, What do you want out of life? What's so bad about what we got?

Q: **What keeps this marriage together?**
SUSAN: Learning to keep your mouth closed at times. I don't know.

PAUL: Tolerance, I think. I mean we don't stew; we have arguments, big arguments like anyone else, and we have spoken about this before. We don't tend to stew over it for any length of time. We can be unbelievable together, you know, biting each other's heads off, but we never go to the next day.

SUSAN: This is one thing that the show's done to us—it makes you analyze things a bit more, you know. Like maybe if the show hadn't been here, we may have split up. We think, Well, we can see what we were like a long time ago, and it brings it back to you. You think, Well, we had this then. Often a lot of people grow apart and can't see what they had originally.

PAUL: I don't think the show could actually hold you together.

SUSAN: No, no. But what it's showing you is what you had in the past.

I can tell quite a few stories here, but the one that really irritates me the most is that when we have an argument, he says, "That's it. Leave me." And I say fine. We've been married for what, thirteen years now or something, and he still says, "You're leaving me." Well, one day I might just pack my bags and go.

Q: **Is there any way you would want to be a father any differently from the way yours was to you?**
PAUL: I'd like to be more contact-close— actual physical, contact-close. My dad and I are exactly the same like that; you know, if we hug, it's unusual.

Q: **Do the two of you have a dream?**
PAUL: I've always wanted to move to the

country. I wouldn't mind a small property, more relaxed style of living, an attractive sort of lifestyle.

SUSAN: We've just been together for so long; we just sort of plod along together. I enjoy his company and he enjoys mine most of the time. I know that he's gonna come home to me every night, I'm gonna have someone there. He's very secure that way.

PAUL: She does put up with a lot. I can't be that easy to live with. I'm not easy to live with.

42 Q: **Tell me what's been happening about work since the last time I saw you.**
PAUL: I've gone from being stable in basically one job, which was the bricklaying. I probably have had about ten or fifteen jobs—I've never really counted them. Although I haven't been sacked from jobs, I just haven't been able to settle. The job I'm in now is the longest I've ever been in a job, which is three years.

Q: **Why can't you settle?**
PAUL: I don't really know. I guess I'm trying to find something that I like doing. You see, I'm interested in the work I'm doing now. Maybe that's why I've been there for three years. But the other jobs, I just couldn't get motivated in them. I mean, I worked hard in them while I was there, but they weren't me.

Q: **What is the job you are doing now?**
PAUL: I work for a sign company, GSA Design and Products, and they're in Victoria. We do a

little prototyping of different signs, like bank ATM surrounds. These days I run between all of the jobs, like filling in with the waterjet cutter. There's a vinyl cutter there, which I'm starting to learn. I've done a little bit of prototyping work there, and sign installation.

Q: **Is this the future for you?**
PAUL: You have to be careful about that. I'm not really sure; I'm not really sure.

Q: **Do you have any ideas of what you'd like to do for the rest of your working life?**
PAUL: I don't know. I think I've got to a stage now where I just want to stay and work. Two or three years ago, I tried to increase my skills

and went back to school and took a carpentry certificate, because I wanted to go out and work as a carpenter. But I basically found there were too many good carpenters out of work for the jobs that were available. So I didn't go too far with that. I was hoping to get in with a builder that I knew quite well, which would have made me feel a lot more relaxed about starting in that trade about forty.

Q: **Is confidence still an issue with you?**
PAUL: Yes, unfortunately. I've learned to live with it, sort of accept it, but I've never really got on top of it fully, which really annoys me. But I don't know what to do about it, though.

Q: **Is that why you like all the animals, the outside? Do you feel comfortable out here?**
PAUL: I think so, yes. I'm more at peace around the horses and the animals. I can be upset, I can be on edge, and I come down to the horses. And within three or four minutes of being here, I've forgotten everything, you know. So it does calm me down.

Q: **Do horses mean a lot to you?**
PAUL: Yes, they've given me a lot. I feel really peaceful with them. It's just very quiet being on horses. And the areas that you tend to ride in are very scenic, very quiet. Sort of like you've gone back in time, I suppose. I don't just enjoy riding; I enjoy coming down and feeding them and that sort of thing. I get just as much out of that as riding them, really.

I come down here nearly every day, especially when we're hand feeding them. Basically, I come down and just have a bit of a chat with them and feed them and put the water in the

bath for them, because I bring the water from home. I cart the water.

A friend of mine talked me into going to Mansfield on a three-day trail ride. I didn't know how to ride then; I was just hanging on to grim death. I was basically the only nonrider up there, and thought, What the hell have I done for three days on a horse? But that's what kicked it all off. In the end I had such a great time up there and I was so relaxed—it felt like I had gone back forty years.

And year after year, I went up there riding. Even when we haven't had the money, we've pained about should we go or not. It's very hard not to, 'cause we just really enjoy it. These days, there's normally quite a few of us that go up—a group of at least fifteen. And then in the last four years, I looked after Poyken, the buckskin here, and then he was given to me.

Q: **Going to Mansfield is the highlight of the year for you.**
PAUL: It is. Actually, about this time of year I go into work and get the foreman's calendar and put a big cross across four or five days and write something like "Paul—Mansfield" on it so they've got notice that I want that time off. It is true, I don't really like to miss it.

Q: **Would you love to live in the outback? Would you like to travel around Australia and live out in the wilds, as it were?**
PAUL: When I was younger, I definitely wanted to move out of Melbourne, and I would have only needed that encouragement from Sue. If Susan had been exactly the same, we wouldn't be here now. And I don't think I would have come back either to Melbourne. I think once

I'd had the opportunity, that would have been it. I think as I'm getting older, I'm more nervous about doing that. Well, my work's changed, and I probably don't really have enough skills to get in a country sign company. So it would be going back to bricklaying, which I'm not keen on doing, and it's wear and tear on the body.

Q: **If you won a lot of money and you didn't have to work, what would your dream life be?**
PAUL: I'd definitely like to go onto a country property with maybe five acres, that sort of thing, and have horses, basically. And then I would, obviously if money wasn't a problem, I'd definitely see about getting the kids lessons, because I mean like all kids, if your parents have got horses or are interested in horses, then they want a horse. And of course, that's the same with my two kids.

Q: **What is it about Australia that attracts you?**
PAUL: I think it's the serenity, the open spaces. It's just such a beautiful country, right down to even barren land. There is something significant about it, there really is. And you know, we haven't really been out in the areas that we went to when I was younger for a long, long time, but that's still something I would really like to do again. But my wife tells me I have to wait till the kids grow up and leave school.

Q: **So how's married life been since I last saw you?**
PAUL: Shocking, shocking!

SUSAN: We had our twentieth wedding anniversary this last Christmas, just before Christmas.

PAUL: Which is a life sentence.

SUSAN: Yes, everyone reckons that we should be out of jail by now. But no, I think we don't change much. Do we?

PAUL: I don't think so.

SUSAN: We still argue, we still spend lots of time together. We enjoy spending time together, and since we've moved to this house because it's a smaller block and we have to walk our dog more, we try and go for a walk maybe one or two mornings or days. And the children are just old enough to leave at home for half an hour or an hour. They'd probably like to be left alone for...

PAUL: ...a few weeks!

Q: **And how are things going with the children?**
PAUL: Good in a lot of ways, but we've had some problems, as well. We do a lot with the kids now, because they play a lot of sports. So generally, either one or both of us, on a weekend we take them to different sports.

SUSAN: I think we said in the last one that Robert had started school and he was having a few problems. And now that he's at high school, the problems do get worse and he just is a square peg in a round hole in the normal, mainstream schools. So we've actually moved him now to another high school, a community school, which is much more relaxed, and as a family unit we are a lot calmer.

Q: **Do you see yourselves, your strengths and weaknesses, in your children?**
PAUL: Robert's more outgoing, like Susan, and

Katie's probably a little more—I suppose you'd call it withdrawn, like me in that respect. But at the same time, they are still different. They have got the characteristics, some of our characteristics, but they've got their own, as well.

SUSAN: You see, because we are such opposites, they are also opposites.

Q: **Does having a marriage of opposites work?**
SUSAN: Well, I think if you had two Pauls together, it wouldn't last—and if you had two of me in a marriage, it probably wouldn't last.

PAUL: She probably brought me out of myself a little bit, and I've probably brought her back a little bit.

Q: **Has he changed in the last seven years?**
SUSAN: Yes, I think so. I think age is a great leveler. It gives you the confidence to do things, you know, like, "I'm a big person now and I don't have to take stuff." In the last seven years, I haven't, but he has, yes, he has changed. He keeps telling me how he's not confident, but sometimes he seems pretty confident to me. Having a go at things.

We're both chatterboxes when we're together. He never used to be; now I've made him talk a lot. He used to sit there and not talk, and I'd say, "For God's sake, just talk to me," and I needed to talk all the time.

Q: **Since I last saw you, you've moved house. Why?**
PAUL: The other one got a bit small, I guess, and we were just after a bit more space with the kids getting older. Thought it would give them a little bit more privacy.

Q: **Do you like it?**

SUSAN: I really like it—it's like living in a palace compared to our other house, because it's nearly twice the size. We'd been talking about moving on and off for ages, and just neither of us had got together at the same time to say, "Yes, I want to move." These things happened and we just decided that that was it. Put the house on the market and it sold in two days, and it was a mad rush to find something else.

Q: **And is it the same sort of neighborhood you were in before?**
PAUL: A little bit different, I think. I think probably a few more professional people live around this area.

Q: **So you moved up the market a bit?**
PAUL: Yes, yes we have. It was an investment thing, too, for later on really, 'cause we got to a point where we paid the other house off. So I suppose it's a form of savings, too.

Q: **Are you comfortable with moving upper class a bit?**
PAUL: I don't think we really looked at it as that. It's just that we wanted a bigger house and it just happened to be in this particular neighborhood. It could quite easily have been in the same neighborhood, because we looked at houses in North Bayswater, where we lived. We just couldn't find one that we liked.

Q: **Will you have to make financial sacrifices to keep it going?**
PAUL: I think we will have to tighten up, because we went at least twelve months where we weren't paying home loan services. Certainly for that reason alone we have to tighten

up a bit. But we will have to watch our purse strings, maybe.

Q: **Is money an issue between you?**

PAUL: We do have discussions, and sometimes we get a little bit heated about whether we can save more than we do, that sort of thing. I think that's pretty standard. We've found it doesn't seem to matter how much people earn—they're still at roughly the same point where we are.

SUSAN: People that have gone to a better wage have often said to us, "The more you earn, the more you spend." You know, it doesn't make that much difference.

PAUL: Really for quite a few years we've lived reasonably comfortably. You know, we haven't really gone out of our way to scrimp and scrape or really knuckle down, so I think if things got a little bit tight, we'd manage to really buckle down again. Which we'll probably be doing shortly anyway, to sort of secure things. Make things a bit safe, you know, for a while.

Q: **You had a very dislocated childhood. What effect has that had on you, do you think?**

PAUL: I'm not really sure, to tell you the truth. I think the initial separation of my dad and real mother might have had more effect on my brother Grahame—he was two years older, so it might have had more effect on him. I might have been a bit more insulated than he was.

Q: **Susan, have you really thought about that?**

SUSAN: Yes, I have. Paul doesn't have anything to compare it to and I did, 'cause I had a wonderful childhood. My father died when I was about nineteen, but I had him most of my life. I had both sets of grandparents, I had a huge family nucleus to always call, and, you know, I think that's why I just skip along in life without that much care, because I know there are always lots of people around me. But Mr. Worrywart here felt very alone a lot of times, and in the early parts of our marriage when we used to have arguments, he used to say to me, "For God's sake, I've got no one else. Don't fight with me!" He hated it, he really hated fighting.

PAUL: I didn't grow up even understanding what an uncle was. It was only Susan's family that sort of tried to explain. I mean, I obviously knew there were relations in a family, but I didn't know exactly what first cousins, uncles, all that was, and I still don't think I know.

Q: **You said something moving last time about what keeps you together—that he's reliable and he comes home to you.**

SUSAN: I keep telling my children, "Isn't it nice to be loved and to know that someone loves you?" It must be really sad for people out there that have no one, that don't know that they are loved. And each day you are coming home and you think, Well, they'll all be home and it's nice to just come home to your family.

Q: **What keeps you going, Paul?**

PAUL: The same thing, I think.

SUSAN: Yeah, we always rush to come home.

PAUL: You're gonna make me cry. I think that's what it is—I think I'm pretty lucky in that respect. Even when times get tough, you know you can go home.

ANDREW

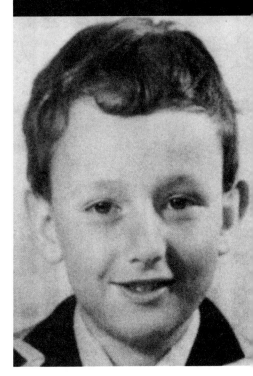

"It was marvelous for a small boy to be able to get out in the open spaces at the weekends and do all the things that you cannot do in London," says Andrew, recalling the cottage in rural Sussex where he and his parents used to spend weekends. "I have loved the country ever since."

When not in the countryside, Andrew lived with his parents in London's South Kensington. His father was a merchant banker and newspaper columnist; his mother owned a hairdressing salon in the West End. Shortly after the filming of 7UP, Andrew, an only child, was sent to a boys' boarding school in Kent. "Although, with hindsight, the education I received there was to stand me in good stead for the future," he reflects, "I did not really enjoy being away from home at that age. I do not think that I would want to send my own sons away from home at such a tender age."

7

Q: **What do you think about the system of house captains at your school?**

ANDREW: I think the system of house captains is rather good, because when somebody is naughty, the house captain asks him and has a talk to him. Once I had a talk with Greville—he was in my house—and I asked Sir if he could put him out of my house, because he was always getting minuses.

Sir said he would see about it this term.

Q: **Do you think house captains should be elected or appointed by Sir?**
ANDREW: Appointed.

Q: **Tell me, what do you think about girlfriends?**
ANDREW: I've got one, but I don't think much of her.

The girls never do what the boys want. They always start playing with dolls when the boys want to play rough and tumble with them. And they always take you away from whatever game you're playing yourself.

Q: **What do you do in your spare time?**

ANDREW: When I go home, I have tea. Then I practice my piano, then I practice my recorder, and then I start watching television.

Q: **What time do you go to bed?**
ANDREW: Well, I have my bath at six o'clock and then go to bed at seven and read until half past seven.

Q: **Do you read the newspaper?**
ANDREW: I read the *Financial Times*. I like my newspaper, because I've got shares in it and I know every day what my shares are. On Mondays they don't move up, so I don't look at it.

ANDREW

Q: **Is paying for schools a good thing?**
ANDREW: I think so. [Otherwise] the poor people would come rushing in and the man in charge of the school would get very angry because he wouldn't be able to pay all the masters if he didn't get the money.

Q: **What plans do you have for the future?**
ANDREW: When I leave this school, I go to Broadstairs, St. Peter's Court. Then after that, I'm going to Charterhouse, and then after that to Trinity Hall, Cambridge.

14 *At fourteen, Andrew was attending Charterhouse, a public school in Surrey.*

Q: **What do you think of boarding school?**
ANDREW: Well, I think boarding makes you feel self-sufficient, and it also teaches you to be away from your parents, and to live with people for a long time, which you have to do in later life anyway.

Q: **How do you spend your free time?**
ANDREW: I'm quite interested in archaeology. We are doing a local dig near our school.

Q: **Have you ever been abroad?**
ANDREW: Not till this holiday have I ever been out of Europe. This holiday, I went to America to stay with somebody from school.

Q: **Do you have any girlfriends?**
ANDREW: They're beginning to become more important. They are no longer just bores.

Q: **Do you not feel you should be meeting a broader range of persons from different backgrounds?**

ANDREW: We do mix with people from the town. When I went to Glasgow and I saw the Gorbals, that rather upset me... to think that people are living in that state when we waste things every day.

Q: **Do you want to be rich?**
ANDREW: Mainly to be self-sufficient—to feel that you don't have to owe anything to anybody.

Q: **Are you religious?**
ANDREW: You have got to believe in something, so God seems to be the most logical thing.

Q: **What do you think about making this program?**
ANDREW: We're not necessarily typical examples, and that's what people seeing the program might think—and falsely. I mean, they tend to typecast us, so everything we say they will think, "That's a typical result of the public schools."

21

At twenty-one, Andrew was reading law at Trinity College, Cambridge.

Q: **Do you think there is any truth in the ideas behind the program that certain people have more options than others and this is undesirable?**

ANDREW: The mere knowledge creates an option in itself. I do think we have more options; it is undesirable, but it is very difficult to correct.

We've been taught to expect more. It's not that because we'd been to private schools, we're better qualified necessarily; it's a matter of expectations.

Q: **What do you think about the concept of paying for education?**

ANDREW: I think if people earn their money, they should have the right to spend it, and education is very important. You can never be sure of leaving your children any worldly goods, but at least you can be sure that once you've given them a good education, that's something that no one can take away.

Q: **Tell me about your ski trips to the French Alps.**

ANDREW: Well, when I was very small, my father always used to go skiing and he took me with him, and we've been ever since, really.

Q: **And how young were you when you started?**

ANDREW: Oh, about five, on tiny little skis. It was quite frightening, really.

Q: **What is the appeal of it?**

ANDREW: Well, the freedom and going in the snow, in the mountains, and the feeling of speed and getting away from people if you can.

Q: **Do you save up to come skiing?**

ANDREW: I don't, but my father does. And he pays for me.

Q: **Your parents have gotten divorced?**

ANDREW: That's right—quite recently.

Q: **Tell me about that and the effect it's had on you.**

ANDREW: Well, not much influence, in fact, because it happened when I'm quite old and I'm away from home a lot anyway. It's very sad, of course, but I don't think it has had a great deal of influence. If it had happened when I was much younger, it would have had much more influence, an adverse influence, I would have thought.

Q: **What are your goals for the future?**

ANDREW: I'd like to be a solicitor and also fairly successful.

Q: **Do you see yourself as staying in England, making your career in England?**

ANDREW: Yes. Well, the trouble with law is it's not very exportable, from my point of view. Anyway, I quite like England.

28 At twenty-eight, Andrew was working as a solicitor in a large London firm. He was married to Jane, who was working full time as a secretary; the couple spent weekends in the Sussex countryside, converting an old barn that they bought with financial help from their parents.

Q: **What qualities do you think it takes to be successful in your work?**
ANDREW: Well, you have to have a legal ability in my business, obviously, and you have to have a sort of bedside manner as far as your clients are concerned. It's no good being brilliant if you can't communicate with your clients.

Q: **Do you think it's bad that people like you opt out of the state system?**
ANDREW: Well, there are really two counter-arguments. First of all, there's the argument that people should have the choice, if they've earned the money, to spend it. And then the other argument is that if we all went to the same sort of schools, those schools would probably be better, because those people who had influence would do their utmost to make them better, if they had to send their children there. Whereas they just look back and don't particularly care what happens in the state system.

Q: **What do you feel about that?**
ANDREW: Well, I think probably the latter choice is fairly impractical, so I suppose one has to continue with the idea of everyone having a choice.

It's a shame that all people can't get the opportunities that I have had. And I'm not sure how one deals with that. I've had all the material advantages, and I've had the opportunity to make the most of them. I have been really lucky.

Q: **Jane, tell me about your background.**
JANE: I don't think I financially come from the same background. Andrew didn't go for a haughty deb; he went for a good Yorkshire lass. But I mean obviously he knew what he wanted.

I think I'm probably quite down to earth. I tend to be less extravagant than maybe some women are who go out and buy lots of expensive dresses. I just go out and buy one or two.

35

At thirty-five, Andrew had become a partner at his law firm. Jane had left her job and was staying home with the children.

Q: **What's been happening since you were twenty-eight?**

ANDREW: I suppose the most important thing that's happened is that we've had two children. One five years ago, Alexander, and then a couple of years later, Timothy. We've also moved out from central London over to Wimbledon. We decided we should look somewhere there was a bit of green space, so we moved out here.

Q: **What was the biggest surprise about having children?**

ANDREW: When I see the children playing together now, I realize how much fun they have together, and it's probably what I missed perhaps being an only child.

Q: **Tell me about your work.**

ANDREW: Well, I work in the corporate department of a large firm of solicitors in the city that is dealing with things like mergers and acquisitions, joint ventures, general corporate advice, putting deals together for clients.

Q: **What are your feelings about the balance between money spent in the public sector and in the private sector?**

ANDREW: The important issue is drawing the distinction between allowing people to spend the money they earn, in other words low taxes, and also putting enough money into the infrastructure—things like education, health service, transport system. And that's a very difficult balance to draw, and I'm not sure that we're doing the right thing at the moment. I think more should be being put into that, and I think perhaps people would be prepared to pay higher taxes to pay for that sort of thing.

Q: **Does money concern you a lot?**

ANDREW: I think so long as one has enough to be comfortable, that's really what one should aim for.

Q: **Is the family unit the most important thing in your lives, more than your own ambition?**

ANDREW: I'm not sure that I have any ambition as such now—just to progress with my work and so on.

ANDREW

42 *Though they still live in Wimbledon, Andrew, Jane, and the boys were filmed on a trip to New York City.*

Q: **Tell me, Andrew, what's happened since we last met seven years ago?**

ANDREW: Well, not really much has changed for us over the last seven years. I'm still in the same job, working for a large law firm, in the city of London. We live in the same house, even have the same car. Our children have obviously grown older: Alexander, our oldest son, is now coming into his teens, and moving school, hopefully later this year. And Timothy, our younger son, is going to be ten.

Q: **How's the work going?**

ANDREW: It's going fine. I suppose the pace has changed a bit; as you know, with technology, people expect work done much faster than they did—well, perhaps not so much as seven years ago, but fourteen years ago. Our practice has got much more international, with more business travel; we have offices in places like São Paulo in Brazil, Moscow, Thailand.

Q: **How has that changed your life, or your part in the company?**

ANDREW: Well, it really means that you are under increasing pressure to produce things quickly.

Q: **And how is that for you?**

ANDREW: That's fine; you have to meet the pressures. That's what people come to your firm for.

Q: **And are you advancing in the firm?**

ANDREW: No, not really. I'm still a partner, and that's really where I shall be until I retire.

Q: **What's the most interesting thing about the work?**

ANDREW: Well, its tremendous variety: you never quite know what you're going to get when you come into work. Different problems and different sorts of jobs arise all sorts of times.

And it's not just looking at what's happening in Britain. You are considering what's happening all over the world—the opportunities for business all over the world.

Q: **How is it keeping the family together and doing a pressured job?**

ANDREW: I think having a family gives you stability at home. It puts things in perspective, when you get home and you find your wife discussing more mundane, perhaps more mundane things...

JANE: [laughing] Thank you!

ANDREW: ...rather than sort of high-powered work type things. That gives you a perspective on life. And also watching your children grow up and go to school and the problems and things that they achieve at school.

Q: **You always wanted to do this job, didn't you? I was looking at** 21UP, **and you said you wanted to be a lawyer, solicitor.**
ANDREW: Yes. Well, at twenty-one, of course, I was just coming to the end of my university career, so by that time, I would have to have chosen what I was going to do, or at least that sort of job. I didn't know when I was seven or fourteen that I wanted to be a lawyer; it's something really that came later.

Q: **Do you have any regrets about the choices you made or anything with work that you would have wanted to have happen differently?**
ANDREW: No, I don't think so.

Q: **Are you involved in his work at all, Jane?**
JANE: Not really, no. I try to understand it, but that's about as far as it goes.

Q: **And do you see that as one of the tasks of marriage, to keep a perspective on his work?**
JANE: Yes. I think so, yes it is definitely, to support him when he's got it, when it's tough, but to also make him relax when a job is over, or you know when it's really bad, just to try and say, "Now come on, let's just get this into perspective." And it does make a difference.

Q: **And you don't feel the need for your own career?**
JANE: No. I left work when I had Alexander, and I decided then that I really wanted to stay at home with the children and not have a career, and Andrew was quite happy with that. I'm fortunate enough that we can have a reasonable standard of living without me working, and I'm happy in looking after them. I don't have any regrets.

Q: **And, Andrew, do you feel the same about Jane? Are you glad she doesn't have a career?**
ANDREW: Well, I think it's really a very personal thing. Some people just feel lost without a career, and Jane wants to be a mother, and one has to respect that. Different people have different yearnings. I don't think you can choose for other people on that.

Q: **Can you imagine not working?**
ANDREW: Not at the moment, but I suppose as one gets older, one can imagine it.

Q: **How's married life together? Is that going well?**
JANE: I think so, isn't it?

ANDREW: Yes.

JANE: Here we are.

Q: **What's the most difficult thing about keeping the marriage together?**
ANDREW: I don't think it is particularly difficult, actually. We seem to manage all right. Would you say?

JANE: I think so. We talk, don't we? We have a situation where we retain a baby-sitter once a week, and we make a point, if at all possible, that once a week, we always go out by ourselves, mid-week, and I think that's quite important. You know, if he's been working long hours, or if I've had a problem with one of the children, it does mean that we've just got no interruption with our conversation, and I think that's been really very important.

Q: **So you make an effort to carve out time.**
ANDREW: Yes. You hear about people who devote their whole life to their children, and when they get into their forties and fifties, when their children have gone away, perhaps they don't have anything to say to each other, because they aren't used to talking to each other. Certainly we don't think we will have that problem.

Q: **We're here in New York. Is this something you try and do, travel and have holidays as a family?**
ANDREW: Yes, we do. It's our children's half-term, so we decided to spend a few days in New York. I come here from time to time on my work, but it's usually very rushed, rushing from an airplane to a hotel to a meeting room and back to a hotel, and then rushing off again. But we thought it would be rather nice to bring them with us, and see it in a more leisurely way.

New York itself is full of vitality, has a tremendous buzz about it, and it's an exciting place to visit. The architecture is wonderful, with these large 1930s and 1940s skyscrapers, reaching up into the sky, sort of like canyon walls.

Q: **And is this something you want to give them, this sense of the world, this sense of travel?**
ANDREW: Yes, I think it is good for them to travel. They say travel broadens the mind. I'm sure that's right.

Q: **What sort of trips have you made as a family?**
ANDREW: Well, we tend to go on our sort of ritual skiing holiday every year, which I drag Jane along for, because she's not terribly keen on skiing. And then we go on a summer holiday, and then the odd weekend here and there.

Q: **You came from a divorced family. Has that made you more attentive, do you think, to family life?**
ANDREW: Well, my family were not divorced until I was in my late teens, so I don't think it really affected me in that way.

JANE: Your parents are still very friendly with each other.

ANDREW: Yes, they are indeed.

Q: **Do you think it gave you, though, a different aspect on what you wanted out of marriage?**
ANDREW: I don't think it has made any difference. I got married in my late twenties, having found who I thought was the right person, but I didn't keep on saying, "I've seen what happened to them, and I can't possibly get married. I must wait to make sure that Jane was the right person." So I don't think it had a fundamental effect.

Q: **What have the children inherited from you, do you think?**
ANDREW: I suppose a reasonably good sense of humor, flexible outlook on life, not being too biased—that sort of thing.

Q: **Are you bringing the children up in the way that you were brought up?**
ANDREW: Yes. My upbringing was fairly easygoing, not too pressurized, and we're trying to do the same with our children. I think it's become much more competitive for children nowadays: they have to sit many more exams than when I was a child. But

again, one must try and not get it out of perspective. As long as they do what they can, that's all you can hope for.

Q: **What have you decided about the education? What are you going to do with it?**
ANDREW: Well, Alexander is coming up into his teens and he'll be sitting common entrance to go to his next school later in the year, which will be a boarding school. In fact, he's down to go to the same school as I went to, which is still a good school and reasonably close to where we live. Timothy is continuing where he is now, for a while, and perhaps will be going through the same procedure.

Q: **How do you feel about the boarding school idea?**
ANDREW: Well, we thought quite carefully about it before deciding. I went away to boarding school when I was seven. And that was really quite a young age to be away from your parents. We decided we didn't want that for our children. I was an only child, so being away at boarding school was perhaps one way of putting me with lots of other children, but we thought once thirteen had been reached, that would be fine, it would be good for Alexander. He's very keen to do it himself.

JANE: Yes, I was going to say, it's really his decision as much as it is ours. I mean, it has been a discussion, and at the end of the day he has decided that is what he would like to do. Whereas I think in the past, probably children were just sent away at thirteen, and they didn't have any question about it themselves.

Q: **Do you have fears for the future with them?**
ANDREW: Yes, I think as a parent, you have all the usual fears—that they'll go on drugs or drop out or whatever, not find their way in life. It would be unnatural not to.

Q: **One of the most powerful images of the film is when you and John and Charles sat there at seven, with your life kind of laid out.**
ANDREW: That's right—born with a silver spoon in your mouth. I think people who have been born into that sort of background obviously have perhaps more opportunities, say to the extent that it's been made easier for them.

Q: **Is that true of you?**
ANDREW: It has been made easier for me, yes, than if I had come from a working-class background, perhaps.

Q: **And how do you feel about that?**
ANDREW: Just a fact of life. Clearly everyone should have equal opportunity.

Q: **But people don't...**
ANDREW: But they don't.

Q: **And that's wasteful, isn't it?**
ANDREW: Yes, it is.

Q: **How would you like to see England change?**
ANDREW: I suppose in an ideal world, greater opportunity for everyone, a wonderful national health service, brilliant education for everybody, so they all got absolutely the same opportunities as each other, that sort of thing.

Q: **You talk about an ideal world. What can someone like you do about creating this society?**
ANDREW: I don't suppose I can do very much, really.

JANE: If somebody comes to you for a job,

you don't judge their background in the consideration of them getting that job.

ANDREW: No, that's true. Certainly, when I'm looking at someone who's applied for a job with me, I wouldn't look at their social background. I would see what they'd achieved and what I thought their potential was.

Q: **Do you have any feelings about the balance between money spent in the public sector and money spent in the private sector? Have things changed over the period?**
ANDREW: Well, not so far, to my mind. More does need to be spent in the public sector still. The health service is desperately short of money still; more needs to be spent on education.

Q: **Is money important to you both?**
ANDREW: Well, if you work hard, it's nice to be rewarded, although I know there are lots of people who work very hard and aren't very well paid. But I think as long as you have a reasonably comfortable existence, that's good enough.

Q: **Is England a class-driven society, do you think?**
ANDREW: Over the years, I think class distinctions have been blurred and people are judged much more now on what they have managed to achieve, rather than what social class they come from. In the city where I work, there are lots of very successful and well-paid people from all sorts of social classes.

Q: **Do you think there's been something inevitable about your progress through life?**
ANDREW: Through life? You know, you look back at us at the age of seven, saying we're going to this school, that university, and so on, so to that extent—but there have been many places where one could have gone wrong. Just because you have the opportunities, it doesn't mean that you necessarily are going to pull through.

Q: **And what is it do you think that's pulled you through?**
ANDREW: Well, I suppose it's just being persistent. I don't like giving up, and perhaps it's also not being too adventurous, not wanting to do anything else once you start, you know. I've been in my job for twenty years; I haven't really wanted to do anything else.

Q: **Would that be a negative, not being adventurous?**
ANDREW: Well, it's served me quite well, as it happens.

JACKIE

The third of five sisters, Jackie grew up in a three-bedroom flat in the East End. "Home was cramped," she recalls. "There were three of us—myself and my two younger sisters—sharing a room. We were always being moaned at to put the toys away because there wasn't enough room." Jackie's family lived at the end of a block, and she remembers that in winter her bedroom used to get quite cold. "Mind you, we had blankets galore—and we had each other to keep us warm."

After school and on weekends, Jackie frequently stayed overnight at the home of Sue, another participant in the UP series, and an only child. "I felt spoilt when I went there, because there was only me and Sue. I know it sounds silly, but you didn't have to share when you went to Sue's."

Though Jackie acknowledges that "materially, mum and dad would certainly have been happier with a lot more," she stresses that her parents "always managed to get what we wanted. I don't know how they did it. Because at the end of the day, they never really had two halfpennies to rub together."

Q: **Jackie, what do you think about boys fighting?**
JACKIE: It's really silly to fight, 'cause if you fight and Miss comes into the classroom, you only get told off.

Q: **What did you think when your baby sister was born?**
JACKIE: My mum's had seven years' bad luck; that's why she's got five girls. And when the baby was about to be born, we all wished it was a boy, but we were all waiting. My dad visited her and he came home and said, "It's another girl, kids." And we said, "Aaaaah!"

Q: **Do you think it's important to help poor people?**
JACKIE: Yeah, 'cause if you don't help them, they'd sort of die, wouldn't they? And every time we have a Harvest Festival, we send food to them.

Q: **What do you think about colored people?**
JACKIE: Well, they're nice—they're just the same as us, really, but one thing: it's only

'cause their skin's brown and we're white, sort of pinkish we are.

Q: **Do you want to get married when you grow up?**
JACKIE: I would like to get married when I grow up. I don't know what sort of boy, but I think one that's not got a lot of money but he has got some money—not a lot.

Q: **What would you do if you did have a lot of money?**
JACKIE: I would buy myself a new house, one that's all nice and comfy.

14 *At fourteen, Jackie was attending St. Paul's Way Comprehensive School, which she chose instead of an academically selective school.*

Q: **What advantages has a comprehensive school got?**
JACKIE: What I enjoy about this school is we do metal work and woodwork and the boys do cookery. We get our share of everything, as it were.

Q: **What do you do in the evenings?**
JACKIE: Go out with friends normally, or to clubs sometimes.

Q: **Have you ever been abroad?**
JACKIE: I've never been abroad.

Q: **Have you got any boyfriends?**
JACKIE: I don't like the way you come out with that!

Q: **Who do you think is to blame for strikes, the workers or the management?**
JACKIE: Say the workers and we'll get loads of letters.
   They're going to strike for it, right? They're going to get more money, the school meals are going up, so that means they're going to strike again. And they're just going to keep on going and going.

Q: **What do you think of rich people?**
JACKIE: Some people are just born into rich families, and they are lucky.

Q: **Do you want to be rich?**
JACKIE: To be comfortable, just so long as you've got all you need.

Q: **Do you believe in God?**
JACKIE: I don't really know if I do or not— I don't really think about it much. That's the sort of thing I'd like to sit and think about, or talk to somebody about.

Q: **What are your ambitions for the future?**
JACKIE: I would like to have a happy family. I mean, it is not possible to be happy all the time, but as much of the time as it was possible.

At nineteen, Jackie married Mick, a decorator whom she met at a local pub. The couple relocated to Essex.

Q: **What was the wedding like?**

JACKIE: It was a funny day, actually. Two of my friends and I were up 'til around five o'clock, and I spent all day preparing—well, all morning, I should say—and then sitting around for about three hours just waiting for something to happen. And when it did happen, I don't remember it happening. It was just complete confusion, really.

Q: **Did anything happen, anything funny?**

JACKIE: I can't forget the cake. It was horrific —really, the wedding cake. It was sitting just between Mick and myself and suddenly the columns gave way and fell into one!

Q: **Do you think you settled down too young?**

JACKIE: No, I've married and we do things together. I mean, I go out on my own sometimes with friends from work. He does the same. I mean, what do you mean by settle

down? If you think that being married as far as we're concerned is a case of going to work, coming home and cook tea for hubby, going to bed, getting up, going to work, you're totally mistaken.

Q: **Tell me about your work.**

JACKIE: I left school and started work for an Australian bank, and I'm still there. I've been there three-and-a-half years now. I've done various jobs within the bank. I started off as a telephonist typist, which was very interesting actually, because of the sort of calls you get. Then I went on to work the NCR machine, which is the actual machine which posts the accounts. And then counter work, dealing with clients' money and things like that.

At the moment, my career is about the furthest thing from my mind. I don't really know what I'm aiming for except getting the house together. That can take years.

Q: **Comparing yourself with Suzy, who stands at the other end of the social scale, do you think you've had the same opportunities as her?**

JACKIE: But the whole thing is you're saying "Do we envy anything Suzy's had?" I mean, I don't know *what* Suzy's had. What's Suzy had that I haven't had? I mean, until I know that, I can't honestly say whether I envy her.

Q: **Well, she's had money and she's been around a lot.**

JACKIE: *I've* got money, maybe not enough, but I've got it.

Q: **Do you ever get depressed about money?**

JACKIE: When you reach the eighteenth day of the month and my mortgage is due on the twentieth, and there's nowhere near enough money in there, I get depressed about it obviously. You suddenly think, Oh my God, what's going to happen? But it gets there. Don't ask me how, but you get it.

28 At twenty-eight, Jackie was working for an insurance company and living with Mick in London.

Q: **What are your ambitions for your career?**
JACKIE: I certainly don't want to stay in the position I am in at the moment for ever and ever. But how ambitious, I'm not really sure. Tends to change as you get older—so just got to wait and see, really.

Q: **As a working-class girl, you don't feel bitter about a society that maybe gives one stratum more opportunities than another?**
JACKIE: I really don't think we even think about it. I don't even think, to be honest, we consciously think about it until this program comes up once every seven years. I do not sit there thinking, "Huh! She was born into money." "He's had more opportunities." It doesn't even cross my mind.

If you've got a comfortable background, then perhaps it can make life easy, but I think you've also seen within this program that it doesn't always work that way.

Q: **Do you wish your parents had encouraged you to choose a grammar school instead of a comprehensive school?**
JACKIE: Most parents would want every advantage that they can get for their child. Now,

whether you class going to grammar school as an advantage is dependent on your entire outlook. If you don't class it as an advantage, then you're not going to push that.

My father got a reasonably good education. He never went to the local comprehensive. But at the same time, I don't think he was too worried which one I decided to go to. I think he probably knew me better than I did, which was that basically I was a very lazy person, academically. And I think I would have found grammar school a push.

Q: **Do you think you married too young?**
JACKIE: I'm not sure I would recommend it, but again you're generalizing. I would say on average nineteen is probably too young.

Q: **Why have you decided not to have children?**
JACKIE: Basically, I would say because I'm far too selfish, and I enjoy doing what I want when I want and how I want, and certainly at

the moment I can't see any way around that. That's not to say that's a forever decision. Some people can make it work; I just don't think I could.

Q: **You don't think you're missing out on what other women have, their stake in the future?**
JACKIE: Actually, that's a terrible way to put it, you know. That makes it sound like you're saying, "All right, great. We're going to have a child—and that's us."

I do feel, to a degree, that yes, I'm missing out, but I also think that I get far more pleasure—or I'm gaining far more experience—by not having that tie.

35 *Jackie and Mick were divorced when Jackie was twenty-nine. At thirty-five, Jackie had had a son, Charlie, whom she was raising on her own.*

Q: **How did you decide to end your marriage to Mick?**
JACKIE: We decided ourselves—I mean, just between the two of us. We knew it wasn't going any further; we both knew, I think, at the end of the day, we would be happier leading our own lives. Whether that involved other people, you know, was to be seen. But you've got to bear in mind we had no children to worry about, so really the only people that were getting hurt by us was us.

Q: **Tell me about Charlie.**
JACKIE: I had a brief but very sweet relationship, the result of which was Charlie. It's the best thing that could have happened to me, and I would never have believed I could've

enjoyed a child as much as I enjoy him. I actually sat down and sort of thought about should I have him or not. I thought about what I was going to do if I did have him. How was I going to keep him? But it comes down to the same old story: the family. My father's only comment to me was, "It is your decision—you tell me what you want to do and we'll take it from there." And they've totally rallied round me. Anybody that wanted to know just got told I was pregnant, I wasn't with the father, end of story. People that know me know the full story and that's all that matters. And Charlie will when he gets older.

Q: **How did you feel about living off Social Security?**
JACKIE: I took a year off when I had Charlie and the state kept me for that year, but I went back to work. To be honest, at the time I pay everything out, I'm not that much better off, but I feel better.

Q: **Tell me about your mother.**
JACKIE: She initially went into hospital for an exploratory operation. They found out she had cancer, although at that stage we didn't know how bad it was. She was ill at the time; they started chemotherapy and radiation treatment, and she was just so bad. Mum badly wanted to come back to the family and the family needed her here. She then spent nine months of hell I wouldn't have wished on anybody.

Q: **What are your hopes for Charlie's future?**
JACKIE: All I am interested in is what is good for me, what is good for my son, and that's it. I don't sit there envying maybe what Suzy could do for her children that I couldn't do for mine. Yes, I'd love the money to put him all round the world, I'd love to be able to do that, but I haven't got it. And at the end of the day, I'm going to do what I can.

Q: **You seem very happy.**
JACKIE: This precise moment in time is probably one of the best times of my life—I think probably because I've got Charlie. He's totally transformed my life. A lot of the times I obviously pull my hair out, but certainly for the better. So yes, I'm a lot happier within myself. People around me have noticed that.

I don't really want Charlie to be an only. I'd love him to have brothers and sisters, but not necessarily loads of 'em—just one would do, actually. I think Charlie would like that as well. I think Charlie would love it.

42

Q: **Tell me, what has happened to you in the last seven years since we were together?**
JACKIE: Well, I already had Charlie when we did the last one. I've since had the other two boys, James and Lee, and moved from London up to Scotland. I've split from the boys' dad, and we're now living on our own, although he is a regular visitor and sees the children quite often. I was working up here till very, very recently, but they've discovered that I've got rheumatoid arthritis, so at the moment that's put work on hold.

Q: **How is it bringing up three?**
JACKIE: Hard work, but obviously very rewarding. It's more than my life. I mean, everything revolves around them and what they need. They give me a lot of pressure, a lot of hassle, and they can be a bit of a pain—but no, they're good.

Q: **What went on in your mind that you wanted three of them?**

JACKIE: I think after having Charlie, it was just a lot more pleasure to it than I ever imagined in London. There was no way I was only having one. I was in a relationship with Ian, and we had James and then we decided that we'd better round this up. Actually, if I am totally honest, I wanted a little girl, which is probably why we had Lee—but we weren't disappointed, not really.

Q: **Which one is the most like you, do you think?**

JACKIE: At the moment, personality-wise, it would be James. He's the cheeky one, he's the one full of confidence. They are all quite like me really, but in different ways. I mean, Charlie is the quieter one: Charlie is the grown-up; he is the more reserved. Lee's an absolute bullet. I mean, if he wants to do something, he just does it—no fear of anything. But they are all good boys. You can
take them almost anywhere.

Q: **Do you bring them up in the way that you were brought up?**

JACKIE: Yes, very much so. It's very much "please" and "thank you." I mean, manners don't cost anything. One of my father's favorite sayings is, "You should do what I tell you, not as I do." And you will hear the boys at one point repeat that back to me, because they hear me saying it.

There is not much that they get away with. I insist on them being in bed at a certain time during the week. There is a certain behavior that I will accept and a behavior that I won't, and they have to conform to that.

Q: **What's the most fun?**

JACKIE: Comments that they make, the little things that they come out with. The sheer unexpected pleasure of them. It's really hard to describe, but they come up with so many different comments.

Q: **And what's the hardest thing about it?**

JACKIE: It's not the luxuries; the luxuries, to be honest, their gran takes care of. It's just the basics: keeping them fed and clothed and making sure they have got decent shoes on their feet and coats on their backs.

Q: **Tell me about your mother-in-law.**

JACKIE: I just don't know where to begin. If I could have chosen a mother-in-law, she was the one I would have chosen. She's great for me, she's absolutely brilliant with the children, and she's always there when I need her. She'll hear a tone in my voice and there she comes and she takes the boys out or takes me away. She's just always there when I need her to be.

If it wasn't for my mother-in-law, I wouldn't be able to live. My children would not be eating and be clothed the way they are without the help from my mother-in-law.

Q: **Tell me a bit more about her character.**

JACKIE: It's really difficult, because she is such a character. I mean last year, year before, she bought a bike so that she could go on bike rides with the children. Now she is not the smallest woman in the world, as she is first to admit, but she really doesn't give a hoot. If her grandchildren are going to go out bike riding, she wants to go with them. And I've no doubt this year it'll be the rollerblades, because they are all on their blades, and she'll probably end up getting a pair and be out blading with them.

She's got a wicked sense of humor. She loves to torment the boys, but in the right way. She spoils them in the right way and she torments them in the right way. Really quite good fun.

Q: **So how did you land up here, in Scotland?**
JACKIE: Well, because the boys' dad is Scottish and it's his hometown. Charlie was five, about to start school, and it was now or never. If we hadn't moved then, I don't think we would ever have done it, but obviously I am glad that we did. There is a lot more here for the boys: they've got a lot more freedom here. I mean, they know when strangers are here, so the children play out and all the neighbors tend to watch.

This is a place called Newmains, which is about a forty-minute drive from Glasgow. This is actually sort of an estate, but just over there you've got a farm. I mean, there is just so much open space. It's just open fields, and as much as the motorway is just ten minutes down the road, you just don't know it. It is really more like a village—I'll probably get shot for that. But the atmosphere is like a village. Perhaps that's the way of putting it. The way the people treat each other and talk to each other, it's more like a village, and that's a good advert, I think. A very good advert. I like it far more than I ever did London.

Q: **How is it for you being away from your roots?**
JACKIE: Well, they're the roots now. Having said that, I miss the family. I miss Dad in particular, but the phone is there and I am constantly on the phone. I go down and they come up when they can. It works—I mean, it's awful coming back. I go down for a visit and I come back and the tears are streaming at the station, but you know, I've got a life up here. All of us do.

Q: **Is it a surprise that it was so good up here for you?**
JACKIE: Yes, in some ways. I think I am probably surprised the boys settled as quickly and as well as they did. The school works absolutely marvelous with them. You know, they sort of took them in, and children can be cruel—'cause Charlie had the London accent then, although he's not now, but he had a London accent—and they loved that accent. That made him a bit different and a bit special, so, yes, it was good. Settled really quickly.

Q: **We always used to talk about how close the East End was.**
JACKIE: Yes, but the East End of London isn't like that any more. People have to lock their doors. I mean, don't get me wrong, most people do here, but the atmosphere is what it used to be in the East End. People talk to you: you can walk up the street and people say good morning to you. You get on a bus and people will have a conversation with you. I used to get on a bus and go to work, or a train and go to work, and normally you wouldn't think to say hello, but they do that here, and that's the big difference.

Q: **Tell me about the sickness.**
JACKIE: It's painful, particularly my hands and my shoulders. It can be almost crippling at

times, but the trouble is it doesn't come on its own. I mean, you get anemia with it, and once you are low like that, anything that's coming along you seem to pick up. So it's crippling in the actual condition, but with anemia I get tired, and that obviously makes life awkward with the children. Along with that comes depression and the hatred of having to rely on people—which makes me even more depressed. So it is completely debilitating, it really is. And unless you have got it or live with someone that has got it, you really would not understand it at all.

Q: **Why have you got it, do you know?**
JACKIE: It tends to be hereditary, rheumatoid arthritis, but it's not in my case. I mean, I certainly don't know anyone with it in the family, not the sort of grans or granddads. We can't find anyone who had ever had it, so we are not too sure what's happened.

Q: **What's the future for it?**
JACKIE: Well, there is certainly no cure. At the moment, they are literally trying to hold it at bay. They are trying to stem it just so that it gets no worse. Whether we are having much success at that, it is still quite early days and I really don't know at the moment. I certainly don't feel that great at the moment, but that could alter—and with the way medicine advances, who knows. I mean, I am still young, and hopefully in a few years' time they may just find a cure. You just don't know. At the moment, work is out of the question. I just can't: I just have not got the energy even to go to work. And the trouble is my hands get swollen and they get stiff, so I certainly can't

type or use the computer as I normally would. Plus the fact that I can't walk very far. I mean, my feet can get sore, and so I just don't know at the moment. It's just wait-and-see at the moment.

Q: **How do you cope with this in your mind?**
JACKIE: Not very well. I mean, you have your good days and you have your bad days. On the good days, I can virtually go through a day and it can be almost normal, but they are the days that I have to watch more than anything, because I do tend to try and do so much, and if I suddenly decide, yes, I can spring clean today, then the following day I can't manage. So it's learning to live with it. It's not trying to beat it; it's just trying to live with it.

Q: **Who helps you?**
JACKIE: At the moment, nobody really. I must admit the social worker is trying to work that out at the moment. The first thing in the morning is bad, so they are actually going to try and get somebody in to get the boys ready for school and take them to school, which will at least then give me a couple of hours to get myself mobile and in working order, as it were.

Q: **Do the boys know that you're not well?**
JACKIE: Yes, they had to know.

Q: **How do they deal with it?**
JACKIE: Quite well. Charlie—he's the sensitive one—he's, "I'll help you with this one" or "Can I do that for you, mum?" Or just where they would normally jump on me, they've had to stop most of that. Lee doesn't really understand, and unless Lee can physically see something wrong with you, he doesn't under-

stand that you can be ill. So he still tends to jump up and down on me and the older ones will say, "No, don't do that." It's only if I physically react that Lee will realize that he can actually hurt me. But on the whole, they are quite good; they cope with it quite well. Charlie does a lot with the younger two.

Q: Can you tell me about breaking up with Ian?
JACKIE: No. No, I can't.

Q: Is it painful?
JACKIE: Yes, and it's not really for public display, so I'd really rather not.

Q: I mean, is it over, or he's around a lot?
JACKIE: Oh, he's around a lot, and particularly after saying I was never having children, I'll never say "never" again. But, I mean, I don't know. See me in seven years and then we'll find out.

Q: How were the children affected when you and Ian split?
JACKIE: When any couple parts—and I don't care how good or how bad the terms are—there is always a tendency for recrimination: "This was your fault," "This was your fault," and blaming each other. It took us a long while to realize just how much the boys were listening to us. They were taking in everything we were saying, and that was wrong because that wasn't anything to do with them. It was a problem between me and him. It wasn't their fault, it wasn't their problem, and it took me a long while to convince those children that they hadn't done anything wrong.

And I must admit that is one thing that I would totally go over again. If I could rerun that

part of my life, yes, because they could so easily have grown up thinking that it was their fault—and it wasn't, in any way, shape, or form. They just happened to be the unlucky victims of it. In fact, I think there should be counseling for couples breaking up, so that you could do it amicably. So that the children don't get any more hurt than they have to be, because that will hurt regardless of how your parents are. But if you can do it without that acrimony, without that blame, then obviously it's got to be better.

Q: Are you finished with men?
JACKIE: No! Finished with men? My God, anyone would think I was eighty. Yes, come back in forty-two years, Mike, and we'll see if we'll answer that one. No, no—I mean, that's like saying you had a bad teacher at school so you don't want any more teachers. There must be some good ones out there somewhere.

Q: And you're on the look?
JACKIE: Well, I don't know about on the look, but I've got enough on my plate at the moment. I mean, it's just enough to cope with day to day and the three boys.

Q: If you could do it again, is there anything you would do differently?
JACKIE: No, I don't think so. Maybe, maybe I would go on for more education than I did. That's the only thing. I mean, I'd like to think that my children will go to college or university. I think that's the only thing I should have done that I didn't do.

When we did the last program, I think a comment my father made at the time was maybe he should have pushed me a little bit harder. And I think that maybe in retrospect he should have done, and that's probably the one thing that I will do with mine that he didn't do with me. I think I should push them just that little bit harder.

Q: **There was so much hope back then, wasn't there?**
JACKIE: Oh, there still is. Don't make that mistake, Mike. I am down and I am depressed about my illness, but I am certainly not down and depressed about my life. Nothing is going to do that. I've got three wonderful boys. I've got a loving family around me. I mean, I'm lucky! There are a lot of people who are a damn sight worse off than I am, a lot of people.

NEIL

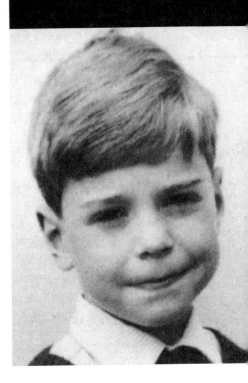

Neil grew up in Woolton, a Liverpool suburb, where he lived with his parents (both teachers) and his younger brother. "I was happy at school," says Neil, "though I can't remember doing a lot of work. I used to play games where you just went off by yourself in the schoolyard and imagined something happening, like America attacking Russia or something like that. You'd be an important character in the story and you'd rendezvous with your mates at the end of it and compare notes."

Neil's father, an avid train enthusiast, used to take Neil and his younger brother train-spotting. Neil's father also organized school trips, often to Belgium. "On one occasion," recalls Neil, "I couldn't sleep on the night train. I was tossing and turning; it was like Christmas eve. So the guard took me into his compartment and told me the names of all the stations. And for somebody who loved trains, this was just so wonderful. Even now, I still get a thrill from traveling on a train, particularly if it's somewhere I haven't been before."

7

Q: **What would you like to do when you grow up?**
NEIL: When I grow up, I want to be an astronaut. But if I can't be an astronaut, I think I'd be a motor-coach driver.

Q: **Tell me about coach driving.**
NEIL: Well, I'm going to take people to the country and sometimes take them to the sea-side. And I'll have a big loudspeaker in the motor coach and tell them whereabouts we are, and what we're going to do, and what the name of the road is, and all about that.

Q: **Would you like to go to university?**

NEIL: Well, I don't think I need to go to university, 'cause I'm not going to be a teacher.

Q: **Why did you say you prefer living in town instead of in the country?**
NEIL: Because in the winter, if you live in the country, it would be just all wet, and there wouldn't be anything for miles around, and you'd get soaked if you tried to go out, and there's no shelter anywhere except in your own house. But in the town, you can go out on wet, wintry days. You can always find somewhere to shelter, 'cause there's lots of places.

Q: **What do you think about fighting?**
NEIL: We don't do much fighting in school,

because we think it's horrible and it hurts.

We pretend we've got swords and we make noises like swords fighting, and when somebody stabs us, we go, "Aargh!"

Q: **What do you do after school?**
NEIL: When I go home, I come in and mummy gives me a cup of tea, and then I go out and play. And when it starts to get dark, I come in again and put on TV.

Q: **Tell me, what do you think about girls?**
NEIL: Well, I hate Caroline Tetford. She's always getting bad-tempered and cross with me. She's always saying, "Neil, move your desk forward." And sometimes when you're supposed to have your chairs back on the desk, she says, "Neil, take your chair forward," and she just gets very cross with me like that.

Q: **What do you think of colored people?**
NEIL: You think of a purple person and red eyes and yellow feet, and you can't really think what they really look like.

Q: **Do you want to have children someday?**
NEIL: When I get married, I don't want to have any children, because they're always doing naughty things and making the whole house untidy.

Although his parents encouraged him to attend a grammar school, Neil chose to attend a comprehensive school in Liverpool.

Q: **Tell me about your school.**
NEIL: When I moved up to a comprehensive school, I found it much bigger, of course, and I found it hard to settle in at first. You get so many different types of people. People with different sorts of brains, you know—from the very clever people to the people who haven't got much sense at all, really.

Q: **Tell me about your interest in chess.**
NEIL: I've been playing since I started at the comprehensive school, since the first year. I think it is a very good idea to have competition, or you relax really and not sort of try hard enough.

Q: **Have you done much traveling?**
NEIL: I used to go with my father; he used to take school parties abroad. I enjoyed Switzerland most, I think. I think it's a very beautiful country, and we went to so many interesting places. I also enjoyed Austria, but not to such a great extent. Those are my favorite two countries. I've been to France and Belgium and Holland as well, but I didn't find them as interesting.

Q: **Would you like a girlfriend?**
NEIL: Perhaps I'm not mature enough yet to
be interested.

Q: **What do you think of colored people?**
NEIL: Well, personally, I've got nothing
against colored people. I think they're the
same as anybody else, but it seems that there
is a lot of argument about them—as any
foreigners, really, that take people's jobs.

Q: **Do you want to be rich?**
NEIL: I think if you are healthy and you have
good friends, you can get on perfectly well.
Everybody would like to be rich.

Q: **Do you believe in God?**
NEIL: Yes, I'd say I believe in God.

Q: **Are you religious?**
NEIL: Well, I go to church with my parents
on Sunday.

Q: **At seven, you said you wanted to be a coach
driver. Have you changed your mind?**
NEIL: It is probably linked up with the fact
that I want to travel. I mean, my thoughts
haven't changed, as I definitely would like to
be a coach driver now.

21 *Neil attended Aberdeen University
for one term and then left school.
At twenty-one, he was doing
casual labor in London and squatting in a London apartment.*

Q: **Tell me about the period in your life when you
went to university and what happened.**
NEIL: Well, I only took university seriously for
a couple of months—two or three months.

Maybe I went to the wrong university or maybe
the university life didn't suit me. Either way,
I felt a very great need to get out of the system.

I did make an application to Oxford, but
I didn't get in. That's in the past now. I don't
know whether I would have been any happier
at Oxford. It had always been a dream to get
into Oxford, I think because people had
encouraged me and because I knew famous
people had been to Oxford. I'd read memoirs
written by famous people, and things like
Brideshead Revisited was a great favorite. But
these, I suppose, were only dreams which I
had when I was at school. I will have to just
get over the fact that I didn't get into Oxford.
Probably because I didn't approach the thing
in the right way.

Q: **Are you bitter about that?**
NEIL: I was very, very bitter at the time. Maybe
I still am, but I try to get over it.

Q: **Why did you come to London?**
NEIL: I came to London because I think I
wanted to start a new life, really. I'd left the

university at Aberdeen at the end of 1975, and I became conscious of the fact that I was still drifting around, which I suppose I'm still doing here. But at least I took the decision to move myself. I think there is possibly more challenge in London than there ever could be in Aberdeen.

Q: **How did you find a place to live?**

NEIL: I came to London and I contacted an agency for squatters, and they were able to give me the address of somebody who was able to help people who were looking for accommodation in the London area. And by process of chasing people around, I eventually managed to find this place. I wouldn't squat in a place which I knew to be owned by somebody else. I wouldn't, because I know that if I had a place of my own and found somebody squatting in it, I would be disgusted; but this place was empty and I was simply offered a place to live and was very grateful for it. I think in questions of squatting, a bit of humanity is more important than vain rules about who can live where.

I've got my own room. I can cook whenever I like; I haven't got a landlady to tell me what time to come in. I've got my own front-door key. To tell you the truth, it's a lot better than a lot of accommodation I've had over the last eighteen months or so. It could be warmer—it's a bit chilly—but it's perfectly satisfactory for the time being.

Q: **What sort of influence did your parents have on you?**

NEIL: Well, they made me believe in God, for a start. I don't know now whether I believe in God or not. I've thought an awful lot about it,

actually, and I still don't know. But still, they made it absolutely certain if one was to survive in the world, one would have to believe in God. It was something that was taught to me. Always think of other people first, before yourself, to a ridiculous, neurotic degree, which I think affected me.

Q: **What do you mean by that?**

NEIL: Well, I suppose it's just basic Christianity, just sort of if somebody slaps you on one cheek, let them do it on the other—almost literally, which gave me a few shocks when I tried to put it into practice.

Q: **In what way?**

NEIL: To go back to that question, I don't think I was really taught any sort of policy of living at all by my parents. This is one of their biggest mistakes: that I was left to myself in a world which they seemed totally oblivious of. And I found even when I tried to discuss problems which were facing me at school, my parents didn't seem to be aware of the nature of the problem.

Q: **Were they ambitious for you?**

NEIL: Yes, but along set lines, which they had planned. They've often said to me that they had seen me even from when I was very young in a certain type of career, and possibly they never even thought that anything else was vaguely possible. They probably imagined I would be maybe a university lecturer or a bank manager or something like that. Some kind of indoor work which involved writing and reading and the rest of the things, because they didn't take into account the other side of my personality.

I wonder how many parents really think of their children as individual human beings.

Q: **What are your feelings about your parents now?**
NEIL: I'm glad they're there, because if I become homeless again, I will be able to go back and live with them. They wouldn't object to this. I'm capable of getting on with my parents perfectly well if they are willing to let me live as another adult in their house and appreciate that I am living my own way of life and that I am living there because I cannot think of anything else to do with myself.

Q: **What do they think of what you are doing now?**
NEIL: They accept it now; they accept the person that I am and they see this simply as my attempting to add more experience to my life, which satisfies me.

Q: **Were they worried about you?**
NEIL: Probably, yes. Well, no more worried than when I first left the university, which was the time when they were most worried. We have, in fact, managed to discuss a lot of personal things which I felt at one time I would never be able to discuss. Therefore, it is possible for me to live for a few weeks, even for a month or so, at home without there being too much friction.

Q: **What goes through your mind when you see those films when you were seven, bright and perky, full of life?**
NEIL: I find it hard to believe I was ever like that—but there's the evidence. I want to know why I was like that. I wonder what it was inside me that made me like that. And I can see even at fourteen that I was beginning to get more

subdued, and I was putting a lot more thought into what I was saying, and to a ridiculous degree. Probably when I was seven, I lived in a wonderful world where everything was a warm sensation and I could be happy one minute and I could be miserable the next minute. I didn't have a plan for the future; I didn't have to worry about having friends. Everything was so mapped out for me.

I don't know what sort of stumbling block should be put in a child's way to get him used to living in the outside world. I think maybe this was something that was wrong with my upbringing: I didn't have enough obstacles to get over to toughen myself up against. I was unprepared for things as they were, but looking back, even now, I couldn't think what might have been done, and I certainly wouldn't start writing educational theories about this, because I know how personal a thing it is and it probably wouldn't work in anybody else's case.

Q: **Would you like to be seven again?**
NEIL: No, because I know I would have to be twenty-one again.

28 At twenty-eight, Neil had just arrived in the Western Highlands of Scotland, following seven years of roaming around Britain. *He was homeless.*

Q: **Tell me about your life over the past few years.**
NEIL: The last three years, I've been unemployed but traveling quite a bit, mostly in Britain. I've been abroad once or twice, but not as extensively as I used to do. I live off

money from Social Security, which does me for my rent and my food. I've been moving about a bit between different places, really. I'm a bit unsettled but I'm very shortly moving to live in digs.

Q: Do you think people like you who live off the state are scrounging?

NEIL: If the state didn't give us any money, it points you toward crime, and I'm glad I don't have to steal to keep myself alive.

I do it simply because I don't want to be without any money at all. If the money runs out, well then, for a few days there's nowhere to go to. That's all you can do. I simply have to find the warmest shed I can find.

The last job I had was cooking in a youth hostel and some cleaning work, as well. I was the only person in the hostel who could speak French, so I used to do a bit of that.

Q: Do you eat every day?

NEIL: Yes, yes, I'm eating better now than I was at times when I was in Aberdeen. In those days sometimes I really was short of food.

Q: How do people regard you here?

NEIL: Well, I'm still known as an eccentric, as I have been since the age of sixteen or so.

Q: Do the days seem long for you?

NEIL: They can do.

Q: Do you have any friends anywhere?

NEIL: I've some good friends still in England.

Q: Do you regret dropping out of university?

NEIL: No formal education can prepare anybody for life; only life can prepare you for what comes, and sooner or later you're going to have to cross certain barriers, and I don't think you ever cross those at school or at university. You come across the problems of mixing with other people, but the real problem, the real problem of becoming a success in the world, is something you have to tackle yourself.

Q: You'd talked about not having enough obstacles in your life. How do you feel about that now?

NEIL: It's funny that, isn't it? I can't remember saying that, but now I do remember and it seems that the whole situation is reversed.

Q: In what way?

NEIL: Now I've got a free hand, but I've got nothing to do with myself.

Q: Do you think you're typical of the environment in which you've lived?

NEIL: I don't think I've been typical of the environment in which I've lived. I might still have been unemployed, but what my background has given me is a sense of just being part of a very impersonal society. The suburbs force this kind of feeling upon somebody. The most you can hope to achieve is to have the right to climb into a suburban train five or ten times a week and just about stagger back for the weekend. The least is just unemployment.

Q: **What other things about modern society turn you off?**
NEIL: The cheap satisfaction of so many things. The aimlessness. But I think the total lack of thought is at the bottom of it.

Nobody seems to know where they or anybody else is going, and nobody seems to worry. You know, you finish the week, you come home, you plug into the TV set and the weekend, and then you manage to get back to work on Monday, and it seems to me that this is just a slow pass to total brainwashing. And if you have a brainwashed society, then you're heading towards doom. There's no question about that.

Q: **It would be pretty tough to convince most people that what you have here, the way you live, the way you look, is better than the suburban life.**
NEIL: Well, I don't want to convince anybody. I know it is. You see, what I look like isn't necessarily what I feel like. I'm not claiming that I feel as though I'm in some sort of Nirvana, but I'm claiming that if I was living in suburbia, I'd be so miserable, I'd feel like cutting my throat. And so there is a slight difference.

Q: **Were your parents upset with what you said about them in the last program?**

NEIL: I'm sure they were, but I don't wish I hadn't said it, because I said exactly what was going through my mind. I think I was venomous, and I think had I been in an easier situation myself, and had I had less worries myself at the time, I would have been perhaps a little kinder. I had to take out my anger on somebody, and I think it came out on my parents. But perhaps unconsciously a lot of what I said was what I did feel underneath. But I don't want the scar to remain.

What I'd like most of all would be to be able to do something for my parents when they're older, to be there when the time is necessary.

Q: **Do you want to have children?**
NEIL: I always told myself that I would never have children, because children inherit something from their parents. And even if my wife were the most high-spirited and ordinary and normal of people, the child would still stand a very fair chance of being not totally full of happiness because of what he or she would've inherited from me.

I know at seven years old, I was fascinated by everything around me—the colors of things that were funny, sounds that people made. I had, if you like, idiosyncratic views about things that other people hadn't even thought about.

I remember I thought that colored people had purple noses and green legs or something like that. Perhaps I'm still looking for the green noses and this sort of thing, and I know that they're still there; I know that when you look at a human being, there's more to that person than just a robot.

Q: **Do you believe in God?**

NEIL: I don't think of God as a creature, but I think of something—time, destiny—which is regulating everybody's affairs, and which you cannot fight against and you cannot order about.

I said to somebody last week that I preferred the Old Testament to the New Testament, because in the Old Testament God is very unpredictable and that's, I think, how I see Him in my life. Sometimes very benevolent, sometimes seemingly needlessly unkind.

Q: **What sort of careers have you thought about?**

NEIL: All the things I always thought I could do. I could give lectures on erudite subjects that I'd read all about, or I could work in the theater, perhaps lighting or directing a show.

Q: **And is all that lost to you?**

NEIL: Does seem to be, yes. I don't see any way out. I've thought of everything I possibly could. It seemed to me for a long time that getting a reliable job, a nice place to live, would be the solution. Well, I haven't succeeded.

I can't see any immediate future at all, but here I am. I've still got clothes on my back, not particularly nice clothes, but I've got them. I have a place to go to; I have some prospects of work. I'm still applying for jobs; I haven't given up. I think I'm lucky because I've met so many people and worked with people who have no future whatsoever, for whom life is finished completely at fifty, and yet they still have to somehow keep going, and I don't want it to seem that I'm complaining too much.

Q: **Do you worry about your sanity?**

NEIL: Other people sometimes worry about it.

Q: **Like who?**

NEIL: As I said, I sometimes can be found behaving in an erratic fashion. Sometimes I get very frustrated, very angry for no apparent reason, for a reason which won't be apparent to other people around me. It's happened from time to time.

Q: **Have you had treatment?**

NEIL: I've occasionally had to see doctors, yes. I haven't had any treatment.

Q: **And what have they said to you?**

NEIL: I've had a lot of advice. But you know the best medicine is kind words, and it usually comes from somebody who has nothing to do with the medical profession, which isn't to say that the doctors can't be very helpful. But really, the thing a sick person wants is to be away from doctors as soon as possible.

Q: **What did they say was wrong with you?**

NEIL: Well, I have always had a nervous complaint. I've had it since I was sixteen. It was responsible for my leaving university and for some of my difficulties with work.

But as you know, you can't afford to go around looking depressed. That in itself is bad enough.

Q: **So can you lick it?**

NEIL: It remains to be seen.

Q: **Do you think, What a waste?**

NEIL: Yes, perhaps.

Q: **Why should you accept this? You're better than all this, aren't you?**

NEIL: No, I'm not better than anything or anybody. I'm just somebody with my own particular difficulties, and my own particular obstacles to surmount, and everybody else is doing exactly the same thing.

35 *At thirty-five, Neil lived in a council flat in the Shetland Islands.*

Q: **Tell me about life here in the Shetland Islands.**
NEIL: The nice thing about here is that you can cut yourself off when you want, because there are people living around, but they're pretty quiet people.

It's an environment which sustains me; it's one in which I can survive. I still feel my real place is in the world, where people are doing what the majority of people do. And the reason I don't feel safe is because I think I'm getting more and more used to this lifestyle, which eventually I shall have to give up.

Q: **How do you manage for money these days?**
NEIL: Social Security still. I wish it wasn't, but I'm afraid it is. I've no desire to be putting the taxes up and drawing money off people who've earned it themselves, but that's the way it is.

Q: **Is the community important to you?**
NEIL: Yes, it has to be. This is where I live. It's been very good to me. People have been especially kind in many areas, and I'd like to be putting something back into it and we'd be putting something back into the whole of Shetland, not just this area.

Q: **Tell me about your involvement with the community theater.**
NEIL: I think the attendance at last year's pantomime on the Saturday night was the biggest crowd of West of Shetland folk I'd ever seen in one place. And you know, we think they enjoyed it.

We had good receptions in other parts of Shetland, as well. We did tour one play. I think we're moving into an age where there's going to be more stress on the community.

Q: **You directed the play last year and you're not this year. Why is that?**
NEIL: Well, the specific reason is that we had a preliminary meeting and my name was not put forward as the one they wanted.

Q: **Why would that be?**
NEIL: Probably because I like to do things in my own way. I'm perhaps quite an authoritative director: I have my own idea of the

performance before we even start, and I don't like people to deviate from that. And during the course of production, of course, people come along with suggestions. No, I accept suggestions; I don't just go along without listening to people. But I know how I want the thing, and once I deviate once from that idea, the whole thing actually falls apart. It's not a work of art anymore. I'm not claiming that I produce marvelous works of art, but I do know what I'm aiming for.

Q: **Do you think of yourself as a writer?**
NEIL: I've had an instinctive feeling I was a writer since I was sixteen. I never really wanted to be anything else. I would actually pay to have something published. I think that's important—there must be something in what I've done. I don't think it's all useless. I probably am overvaluing it, but I know how much effort went into some of it, and on that strength alone I just can't believe it's useless.

With each successive play I don't know who I am trying to speak to and what I'm trying to say to them and whether they're listening. I just keep going, 'cause that's what I feel I should be doing.

Q: **There was an enormous reaction to you in the previous film. What do people see in you, do you think?**
NEIL: It's seeing I was representing some kind of successful escapism or somebody who'd managed to be totally himself, hadn't given in to pressure of society to conform. And people flooded me with letters and seemed to think I could solve their personal problems. And I was quite frightened,

because I knew I couldn't. But what really bothered me was people seemed to see something in me that I hadn't been aware of myself. All I was aware of was that I didn't have anywhere to go. I had nothing to do, I'd no money, I felt let down by quite a lot of people. I didn't think my life was a success, but suddenly everybody seemed to think so. But the most nagging thing was that even if a million people had written to me, it wouldn't have made any difference to my situation.

Q: **Are you having any medical treatment for your mood changes?**
NEIL: No. I haven't for many years, because I wouldn't like to be dependent upon man-made substances for a cure.

Q: **Do you ever think you're going mad?**
NEIL: I don't think it. I know it. Well, we're not allowed to use the word "mad" here, but I think it's a mad world. I think I remember walking into London twelve years ago and just walking through the city, and they were digging up the drains and there were cranes knocking down buildings and there were cars trying to get down impossible alleys and having to reverse out again and policemen trying to do all kinds of things. And I thought, This world is just mad, you know. This world is just mad.

Q: **And how's God been treating you?**
NEIL: Well, after I'd tried about every remedy one could possibly think of for my personality disorders, I thought, Well, I'm going to trust God, because other people have done so, seemingly with positive results. I can't say the moment I trusted God my life was fine, and I

can't say all the time that I think I've found the answer, but I can say with some certainty that once I started believing that there is actually a God who has something of a design for the world, who is working in a certain way in the world, after that, some things became clear to me. I really can't say much more than that.

Q: **What are you likely to be doing in the year 2000?**
NEIL: That's a horrible question! I tend to think most likely the answer is I will be wandering homeless around the streets of London, but with a bit of luck that won't happen.

I always feel that somehow a good fairy has waved a wand over me and saved me from that, because that seemed very much what the end would be for a while. That's why I cling on here. I know how tempting it is to escape into fantasies, to believe that I already am a successful writer, to believe that I've got lots of friends, to believe that if only I had done such and such my life would've been different. But, I mean, the most difficult thing is to accept the reality, to be what we are in a situation. That's terribly difficult.

42 *At forty-two, Neil was living in London and serving as a local councillor, an unpaid elected office. He had also forged a friendship with Bruce, a participant in the UP series.*

Q: **Tell me what's been happening since you were in the Shetlands.**
NEIL: I left Shetland very soon after the last program was made and I moved myself to London. And with the help of Bruce, I was able to find some accommodation—first of all in the Dalston area, and then I moved to a part of Hackney, and since then I've been on a number of training courses. And I did an Open University degree; that was perhaps the longest of all.

I also trained to be a teacher of English as a foreign language in the first year I was in London. I haven't been able to put that to a great deal of use, but I have done a small amount of teaching intermittently. I've done a fair amount of work with the church and various courses, such as parish visiting, befriending. At the moment, I am on what's called a training course to become, hopefully later this year, a reader in the church.

I'm a local councillor, which in fact can be as much a full-time job and more and involves me at the moment most evenings and weekends. But I haven't had paid work apart from a couple of interim government schemes. I worked for a local community theater for about six months, and I worked as a gardener. I suppose everybody my age who has been unemployed anytime has had to work in a garden or a park at some time, and I did my stint. But after about six months of that, needless to say, I did tire of that. It wasn't what I wanted to do as a career, and so I moved on to something else.

Q: **It's like a million miles from Shetland here— the city, the noise, and all that. How have you coped with that?**
NEIL: That is one aspect with it. Certainly, adjusting to London after all that period away —even though I had been back occasionally for visits—was extremely difficult. It became progressively easier. The first six hours were an absolute nightmare, and then the first week was pretty bad, and I suppose it took me a year or so to adjust. But people here have a strong sense of a need for a community—of doing things in groups, of organizing themselves, of progress and change coming up from the street level, if you like, rather than being dished down to them from above. So there are many similarities in that extent, and I found settling to Hackney from a social point of view not as difficult as I expected.

Q: **What's the most fun living in the city?**
NEIL: Obviously for me, the availability of theaters and music, which I'd never had at any other time in my life. It can be a bit tempting sometimes when limited money is available, but that's great. For someone who enjoys travel, being in the hub of the country's travel network is very useful and also the closeness to the continent.

Q: **And what is the hardest thing for you about living in London?**
NEIL: It can be such a lonely place, and I don't think intentionally, but I think people pass on their feelings of grudge and dissatisfaction with their neighbors just through their daily interaction with others. And sometimes there are days when everybody seems to be in a bad mood and it's impossible not to feel that. Of course, this can happen in the country as well, it's just as possible—but I think people in cities need to make a special effort to be aware of other's needs, given the social pressures and how people live so closely to each other.

Noise, of course, can be a terrible pressure in cities, and a lot of duties I have had to perform as a councillor have been trying to solve noise problems. If only people would be a bit more concerned about their neighbors' feelings, so much would be a lot easier. This is where no councillor, no government, and no police force can make the difference. It's a question of individual awareness, and I think if people want to be treated fairly themselves, they have got to try and treat other people with respect. I think that's quite important.

Q: **Do you feel more at ease in company and in groups of people than before?**
NEIL: Oh, I have never felt at ease with groups of people. I'm not a natural socializer, and I'm particularly nervous at social gatherings, like parties. This is well known to my friends, and they don't expect me to be the star of the show. But I think having not had a

regular job for any part of my life or length of time inevitably makes me very unfamiliar with the sort of social behavior that is natural for so many people. Perhaps that's not so much a personality difficulty as just simply a lack of contact with the world that so many people share.

Q: **When did you become a councillor?**

NEIL: It was in June 1996. A vacancy occurred in a seat which the Liberal Democrats held. Our councillor had to resign owing to work pressures, and, as I had just moved to the ward in which the by-election fell, I was asked would I be the candidate.

Q: **What does your work as a local councillor involve?**

NEIL: Councillors, of course, run councils, take the decisions regarding the budgets, the provision of services, and so forth. This is a job which councillors of all parties are involved in, not just those who are actively leading the council. In our council, there is no party leading; we are under no overall control. But a great proportion of my work, and I would hope for most Liberal Democrat councillors, is actually dealing with members of the public, trying to step in where they are dissatisfied with the services they are getting from the council.

One of the advantages of being a councillor is that a councillor can prioritize his time —and I don't have to do anything at any certain time, apart from attend meetings. At what times a day I do my casework and visit people and so forth is up to my own decision. So I find that a great help.

Q: **What is the most rewarding thing about being in politics for you?**

NEIL: It's being able to help people, to sort out and solve problems which previously we thought unsolvable. I can't claim I've always been able to do that, and I don't think there is a councillor anywhere who can, but it's great, with the help of council officers, of course, getting to grips with the issue and finding out it's not as complex as it originally seemed, and discovering the lines of communication through which one has to work and getting something done.

Recently, I managed I think to get a floor retiled for a lady who has a disabled lodger in the house, and I am so pleased, because normally this is not something I think the council would have done. But because of the circumstances, I was able to intervene and have this work done. And I think this is what councillors in their functions—certainly as representatives of those elected—are there for. I think if somebody has paid rent year after year and been a model tenant, then they deserve good services from the council. It's important.

That is one side of being a councillor. The other side is the policy-making in the council chamber, and they are both important. I don't think anybody can be a satisfied politician if they are not fulfilling both parts of the job.

Q: **Do you have any nerves when you stand up and give speeches or make arguments or defend positions?**

NEIL: Yes, of course, and if I didn't it would be wrong. The councillor who has no nerves is not doing his job. It becomes slightly easier after the first time, and I'm glad you didn't record my first speech, because most of the chamber walked out, and I was determined, like Disraeli, to say something like, "Well, you're not listening now, but one day you will hear me!" But unfortunately, most of the chamber had already walked out.

I do enjoy the rivalry and the competition, and it's a great thrill to be able to change the course of a vote. That's not always possible, but sometimes one can achieve that.

Q: **You're going to have to move up for re-election shortly?**
NEIL: That is correct. In fact, I think by the time that this film is shown, the election would have taken place. So who knows what the result would have been, but yes, I am hoping to stand again. I haven't been re-selected yet, but this procedure comes up in the near future.

I hope I will be re-elected; that depends on my performance in the last two years.

Q: **One thing I keep hearing from you is this word "community." Is that something by which you live?**
NEIL: Yes, the community is important. I have had so many times in my life when I have been on my own and felt vulnerable, and although perhaps this was partly as a result of a seeking to escape from established networks and organizations, I feel that communities must have a sense of truth within themselves. And a community is not a community if it's simply people continuing and being there because they are there.

When it's a religious community or otherwise, there has to be a sense of common

purpose of some kind. This doesn't mean conformity to me and setting a patchwork of laws and rituals, but it means respect and recognizing the importance of others. If there were not people emptying my bins and the neighbors', the street would be filthy. If there were not people driving buses and trains, I wouldn't be able to get anywhere. If there were not people developing new programs at universities, the world would be more restrictive. Whatever people are doing, they are contributing to community. And this is true on a wider level and it's also true on a local geographical level.

I see a huge globe full of individual communities which are serving together side by side—not repressing but learning from one another—and where people recognize other people's cultures and values different from their own and also flourish themselves. I think that is the only way.

Q: **Is the church still an important part of your life?**
NEIL: Going to church is a regular weekly event. I have religious beliefs, which obviously find a ground on my visits to church. Probably I know more people in Hackney through the church than through any other means. And I do see the Christian faith, which has survived changes in custom and rule and invention in science and so forth, to be the center of so much. Of course, the church is no longer the center of society, but I don't see any reason why it still shouldn't be highly significant in individuals' lives.

Q: **And how has your health been?**
NEIL: My health has been a lot better more recently than other times in my life. Maybe

being busy has been the cure. I think my Christian faith has helped me, and I also believe that my friends who have been so loyal and got to know me better and better have been able to show support and sympathy in the most appropriate ways. I do so value the support of friends to whom I can turn. And I need that help.

I think at Shetland I was cut off from a lot of people who over the years have been able to help, but I didn't meet many new friends there. So perhaps just being amongst some of my longer-term friends made a difference.

Q: **How are things with your parents?**
NEIL: Well, my father wasn't so well recently. From what I hear, he's made something of a recovery. Both my parents have now, of course, retired. Still living in the north of England. I think they are as well as could be hoped for.

I've no doubt they were very pleased when I was elected onto the council, and I know they were very pleased when I achieved my Open University degree. There was no stopping them coming to the ceremony, and I was very glad to have them there. So yes, they have been able to participate in some of my successes.

Q: **So how do you do for money?**
NEIL: Well, I was a little better off when I first became a councillor, because apparently the benefit agency had miscalculated how much they should take off my income support. But I've been told I don't have to repay the amount they have overpaid me, and I must say that it wasn't that much as a result of their blunder. So probably I am slightly better off, but the measly amount they give me nowa-

days wouldn't support anybody, and of course if I lose my seat on the council, I would either get a job, which would be preferable, or try to get back onto some reliable benefit. I would much prefer to get a job.

Q: **And why can't you or haven't you gotten a job?**
NEIL: I think I am a bit wiser about that now than I was for a long time, because quite recently I sat on an interview panel, interviewing somebody to work for the council. I discovered so much about interviewing technique, and I think I realize why I had never been successful in any. But what is interesting is that through the countless training sessions I have been on, organized by the employment services and so forth, I have never once been given the adequate tips for passing interviews.

Q: **What are your biggest regrets looking back on your life?**
NEIL: Well, I think not having been married is perhaps one of them. I think not having been able to visit certain places in the world, although I shouldn't be ungrateful because I have traveled a great deal in Europe. Not having been able to publish a single thing I have written or have a single play performed —and I say this despite having moved in circles in which one would have thought this might have become possible.

Q: **Do you feel more useful than you have before?**
NEIL: I feel I am achieving some good on the council. But politics at any level is restricted by the fact that it is only a game of grabbing things, either for yourself or for other people. I don't think it's the highest level in which

individuals or groups can work, and it's certainly not what I feel to be my natural medium.

While I was in Shetland, I felt very strongly that I should become involved in politics simply because I felt I wasn't achieving anything in the ways I really wanted to, and I could see decisions being made politically by people I felt were not competent to make them and who I felt were not representing the majority of the public, and I felt angry. And I felt in my own small world I had to get in there. I think more people should—it's only apathy which leads to bad government at any level. But I still don't feel that I am achieving things in the field in which I want to achieve, and that's in the world of literature and theater.

Q: **Do you think you have changed in the last seven years?**
NEIL: Well, it's always impossible for me to know. I've always been determined to do what I thought was the right thing to do in any situation, and I don't perceive any change in that.

Q: **Is this a good time in your life?**
NEIL: Yes, probably I've never been busier and I've never been in contact with so many people, so I have to say that. Yes, and I feel incredibly grateful for the opportunity to do what I'm doing and grateful for people that elected me. I hope I won't let them down any time. I'm glad that there are some people out there who actually feel I am capable of doing something publicly, because as you know, my persistent failure at interviews for work has inevitably persuaded me that there isn't anybody that wants to use my services.
So it's a great compensation when there are so many hundred people in my ward, saying, "We have the confidence in you."

Q: **What is the most enjoyable thing for you in life at the moment?**
NEIL: I think it's looking to the future.

EPILOGUE

Thirty-five years after the UP series began, Michael Apted asked participants to reflect on the personal impact of appearing in the films.

SUE: It's funny, because before the films start, you think, What on earth have I done with seven years that I can possibly say? What can I talk about that I've done? And you panic. You think, I should have done something. I should have done something dramatic! You know, I was hoping to win the lottery last night, so that I could come on and say so. But life's not like that.

NICK: We were talking about my ambitions as a scientist. My ambition as a scientist is to be more famous for doing science than for being in this film. But unfortunately, it's not going to happen.

NEIL: I've met some of the most interesting people I know, and I'm still in contact with. And this includes people in different parts of the world. And one or two particularly close friendships have been forged through the program. Although I have to say, I was very suspicious when the initial contact was made.

JACKIE: I don't think I'd ever have kept a record of my life in the way that we have with this program. So, yes, I enjoy doing it. But it's not something that takes a great precedence.

ANDREW: If you came and asked me if you could do this to my children, I certainly wouldn't be enthusiastic. I think it's something that I wouldn't want to wish on someone, particularly.

SYMON: I think for the first forty-odd years, it restricted me. Because I was always shy to start with, and knowing that people were going to be looking at me and watching me, rather than do something that's going to look stupid, I've always pulled myself back.

SUZY: There's a lot of baggage that gets stirred up every seven years for me that I find very hard to deal with. And I can put it away for the seven years, and then it comes round again, and the whole lot comes tumbling out again, and I have to deal with it all over again.

BRUCE: It hasn't changed my choices in life. I haven't thought, Well, I have to be doing this by then, or How will this seem to others, or so on. It's just a kind of periodic little intrusion.

TONY: It's the only time, when you're a cabbie, instead of you picking up a celebrity and saying, "Hello. You're, say, for example, Paul Gasgoine, ain't you?" They go, "I know you," and they turn the tables on you, you know?

PAUL: Being honest, I think despite all the things that I might have said over the years about, "Oh no, they're coming in," there is a certain amount of excitement there, too, underlying. I'm old enough to admit it now, I suppose. It probably is a bit of good fun.

LYNN: Some of us don't see family from one year to the next, seven years on, and I think that's how we all feel about each other: We're linked. And that can never go.

11. July. 2000 Book Soup 16.⁹⁵ 77972